3-15-10

Lancelot
5-21-10

HIP HOP IS NOT OUR ENEMY
FROM A PREACHER WHO KEEPS IT REAL

Dr. Kenneth T. Whalum, Jr.

authorHOUSE®

AuthorHouse™
1663 Liberty Drive
Bloomington, IN 47403
www.authorhouse.com
Phone: 1-800-839-8640

© 2010 Dr. Kenneth T. Whalum, Jr.. All rights reserved.

No part of this book may be reproduced, stored in a retrieval system, or transmitted by any means without the written permission of the author.

First published by AuthorHouse 2/17/2010

ISBN: 978-1-4490-7426-5 (e)
ISBN: 978-1-4490-7424-1 (sc)
ISBN: 978-1-4490-7425-8 (hc)

Library of Congress Control Number: 2010901543

Printed in the United States of America
Bloomington, Indiana

This book is printed on acid-free paper.

CONTENTS

Dedication	vii
Introduction	ix
1. We Need To Stop Frontin'	1
2. What Are We Afraid Of?	4
3. What Is Hip-Hop Anyway?	9
4. A Challenge To The Church	13
5. Hip-Hop Is More Than Music	15
6. We Compartmentalize All The Time	19
7. Don't Let The Devil Win!	25
8. We Don't Have Much Time	33
9. Not Ready To Make Nice	35
10. Fake-Phony-Boloney-Pseudo-Semi-Saints	38
11. Shake That Laffy Taffy	41
12. Especially Wicked Sinners Have Wisdom Too	44
13. If Hip-Hop Isn't The Enemy Who Is?	50
14. A Word About Holy Hip-Hop	54
15. Church Is More Than A Social Gathering Place	62
16. Let's Go Deeper	67
17. What Is Your Church's Vision?	71
18. Well I'll Be BAMM'd!	75

19. The Black Church: A Sleeping Giant!	80
20. You've Got To Pay The Piper Whether You Dance Or Not	84
21. Have You Had Your Spiritual Prostate Exam?	91
22. What Kind Of Army Are We Releasing?	94
23. Walk It Out!	99
24. Hip-Hop Theology – How To Preach A Keeping-It-Real Sermon	103

DEDICATION

- Ms. Laura Huggins (aka "Honey"), for your dedication, loyalty, and excellence in the work of transcription.

- The Olives of The New Olivet Baptist Church. Because of you, I can continue to make it do what it do.

- Reverend Tiffany Newby and Mrs. Phyllis Dandridge, the best Administrative (Add To The Ministry) team ever!

- Dr. Paul Dekar, my Missions professor at Memphis Theological Seminary. He made the following statement in class one evening, and it changed my life: "It is the responsibility of the Church to bring her resources to bear on the problems of the world." Thank you, my friend.

- My most beautiful Mother, Mary Helen Pettis Whalum Rogers. You were my very first and biggest fan, and even when I was a baby you shielded me from groupies and the paparazzi☺. Thank you for dressing me up in my Easter suit, even when it wasn't Easter, and making me sit on the porch while everybody else played football. You told me my knees were "too pretty to mess them up" and I still believe it! Momma, you deserve every blessing, every reward, and every comfort you get. When you were born in Senatobia, Mississippi that city was known as "The 5-Star City". When you left they were down to 4!

- The memory of my anointed father, Kenneth Twigg Whalum. (I never say "Sr." because he would pitch a fit about that. He would always say, "I haven't changed my name. Just because you're 'Jr.' doesn't mean I'm 'Sr.' I'm the one and only!") Daddy, I love you. Thank you for my signature. Thank you for my boldness. Thank you for my independence. Thank you for my swagger. Thank you for my freedom. I'm the new YOU!

- My brothers Kirk Wendell Whalum and Kevin Henry Whalum. Thank you for guarding our father's legacy so well. May God continue to bless you, your wives, and your seed.

- Kenneth Twigg Whalum III, my firstborn son. I love you and your music with all my heart.

- Kortland Kirk Whalum, my second-born son. I love you and your music with all my heart.

- Kameron Timothy Whalum, my third-born son. I love you and your music with all my heart.

- Sheila Lee Whalum, my Queen. From the day I first saw you sitting there smiling in the choir stand at Shady Grove Baptist Church, I have been enamored with you. After all these years you still make my teeth itch. You make me want to be better and do better every day. It is an honor to have been chosen to spend this life with you. Thank you my Baby.

- To every school teacher I ever had, especially the ones who wouldn't let me be average. (And especially Mr. Harris, who said – after I failed an exam because I wasn't prepared to take it – "I don't give a damn if your name *is* Whalum, you're going to study in my class!").

INTRODUCTION

PAUL R. DEKAR*

In the United States and around the world, a new Christianity is emerging. Contemporary Christians are adapting cultural forms, creating new genres of worship and democratizing access to the sacred.

Just as musical innovation fueled and sustained the reformations and revivals of the twelfth- sixteenth- and early twentieth-centuries, a vehicle of today's religious reconfiguration has been a tsunami of musical innovation, including hip-hop and rap (terms often used synonymously). Marked by rhythms and lyrics that pulse with life, the hip-hop genre eruped during the 1970s from the so-called secular world, specifically from abandoned places of inner city America, predominantly among especially gifted, motivated and loved black and latino men and women. Many rap and hip-hop artists have been churched. More characteristically, they have felt the wrath of ecclesiastical traditionalists and hierarchs.

Whether in politics or religion, paradigm shifts and revolutions rarely occur cleanly. Thus not all that comes under the hip-hop umbrella is benign. There is good reason that many Christians have taken offense. Yet a different perspective is needed. In this significant jeremiad, Kenneth T. Whalum, Jr. offers a more balanced approach.

Whalum differentiates what is good and what is not in hip-hop, and why Christians need pay heed to the artists and those impacted by the art. Whalum is open to the sensibilities of hip-hop artists, their energy and the possibilities they offer for cultural renewal and religious realignment. Believing "hip-hop is not our enemy," Whalum invites readers to pay attention to, and reflect on the real world of hip-hop. He writes, "The grim reality for a lot of kids out there living alone is that life is harsh and cold; kids grow up faster than they want to because they are forced to!" (p. 52). Many of the songs young people listen to mirror their real world, things they dream about and the fantasies they have. His advice? Do not change the songs young people are listening to. Rather, change the circumstances from which the music has emerged, then the situations and the music will be better!

Along with other reformers, Whalum finds parallels with Jesus and earlier generations alert to the creative language and dynamics of their times. He sees hip-hop artists as embracing their world while believing another world is possible. He invites readers to join the struggle for a better world in this significant arena. Words of the chorus of "new world" by David Wilcox, a musician of different genre, come to mind:

> New world - big horizon
> Open your eyes and see it's true
> New world - across the frightening
> Waves of blue
>
> The old world had attractions
> But hunger in my soul

> Resumes and power plays
> Where lust was just control...
> (David Wilcox, *Big Horizon*, 1994)

Born and raised in the inner-city of Memphis, Tennessee, Whalum knows of what he writes and speaks. Brother of world-renowned tenor saxophonist Kirk Whalum, and father of emerging music stars, Kenneth Whalum, Jr. is a musician in his own right. A cum-laude graduate of Morehouse College in 1978, Temple University School of Law in 1981 and magna cum-laude graduate of Memphis Theological Seminary in 2008, Whalum has dedicated his life to proclaiming social justice for the citizens of Memphis, Tennessee, especially those who cannot speak for themselves, including musicians who speak through the medium of hip-hop. He serves as pastor of The New Olivet Baptist Church, a megachurch in Memphis with dynamic ministries in the arenas of youth and economic empowerment. Reflecting these dual commitments, Whalum has articulated a role for Christians outside the walls of church buildings; in 2006 he won an overwhelming victory as an at-large commissioner of the Memphis City School Board.

In multiple roles (faculty advisor, friend, worshipper) I have known Whalum for some fifteen years. Consistently he has expressed concern not solely about Christian faithfulness, but also that Christians open their eyes to the real world in which many young people live. While the intended audience for <u>Hip-Hop Is Not Our Enemy</u> is the black church, where many pastors and lay persons denounce hip-hop, his study deserves a wider readership. Inevitably where there is smoke, there is also fire.

---

*Having retired in 2008 after a 33-year teaching career Paul R. Dekar is an independent scholar, peace activist and chair of the National Council of the Fellowship of Reconciliation, birth mother in 1939 of the Baptist Pacifist Fellowship. His most recent book is <u>Building a Culture of Peace: Baptist Peace Fellowship of North America , the First Seventy Years</u> (Eugene: Wipf and Stock, 2009).

CHAPTER ONE

WE NEED TO STOP FRONTIN'

In March of 2006, ThreeSixMafia, a rap group from Memphis, Tennessee made history by becoming the first rap group in the Academy Awards' seventy-eight years of presentations to be nominated for an award *and* perform at **The Oscars**. But group members DJ Paul, Juicy J, and Crunchy Black (yes, "Crunchy Black"!) did more than perform on that night's telecast. They actually won an Oscar for *Best Song in a Film* for a tune entitled, of all things, "It's Hard Out Here For A Pimp", which was the theme song from the soundtrack to the movie, "Hustle & Flow".

ThreeSixMafia's victory set off a maelstrom of cultural criticism from respected Black religious leaders and others who objected vociferously to such an iconic and uniquely American honor being bestowed on this peculiar collection of young urbanites. A popular Disciples of Christ Pastor in Memphis opined in a local daily newspaper: "ThreeSixMafia are pawns of the devil", and called on his congregation to mount a "holy war" against their music. He also called on parents in his church to go home and destroy all their children's hip-hop music by breaking their CD's and erasing the music from their iPods!

The upshot of this and most other criticism is that hip-hop music is the source of most of the evils in society, particularly in the Black "community". The terms "rap" and "hip-hop" were used interchangeably in these critiques, as if there were no difference between the two. These modern-day *Joe McCarthy's*, these self-proclaimed keepers of the flame of religious tradition, seemed to revel in their opinion that hip-hop is the root of all evil in the United States today. Shrill voices from all over the religious community suggested that hip-hop is an enemy to be resisted at all costs.

I beg to differ. Hip-hop is not our enemy. Hip-hop is merely one manifestation of our culture. It is easy to blame our culture for the condition of our children, and to blame our children for the condition of the culture, but the Bible says, "And you fathers, do not provoke your children to anger, but bring them up in the discipline and instruction of the Lord." (Ephesians 6:4, KTW Translation). Our responsibility goes way beyond judging our children's actions, and condemning the children for who they are and what they do.

It is easy to condemn ThreeSixMafia and other "gangsta" rap groups because of the lyrics of some of their music. It is easy for us to condemn ThreeSixMafia and other "gangsta" rap groups because they wear gold "grills" in their mouths, but our people have worn gold in their mouths for as long as I can remember. So if the church is condemning its own young people for being who they are, what role does the church play in making them who they are, and what do we have to offer them as an alternative to who they are?

Yes, it is easy to be self-righteous and condemn our children for turning to whatever alternative they see as their only means of escaping poverty. And, trust me, hip-hop culture has created many millionaires of men and women who probably would have spent their lives in abject poverty otherwise.

Black folk (and, by the way, I actually prefer to use the term, "Black". You may prefer "African-American", which is fine with me. We both know of whom we speak!); anyway, Black folk have had churches on every corner much longer than we have had hip-hop music. Our children have been coming out of broken homes much longer than ThreeSixMafia has been at the top of the charts. It is easier to condemn them to hell for calling women "bitches" and "hoes" than it is to stop "fronting". We in the church, so-called leaders in particular, have arguably been given implicit permission by the communities we serve to put up a front and maintain a certain image while actually *treating* women like "bitches" and "hoes".

What it amounts to so often is that we in the church are being hypocritical, saying one thing and doing another. The sad thing is that there are so many young people in our churches who, like many of us, are being nurtured in this traditional mindset, looking down on other folk because they do not look or act or "do church" like we do, yet we are doing the same things we condemn the rappers for doing. Jesus upbraided the cities, he condemned the cities, and he chastised the church folk of his day. They killed him to protect their vested interest.

CHAPTER TWO

WHAT ARE WE AFRAID OF?

What scares us when we look at hard-core rappers like DJ Paul, Juicy J, and Crunchy Black? What frightens us when we look at young men like the one on the cover of this book? **(Would it surprise you to know that at the time of this writing the young man on the cover on this book was a music scholarship student at Morehouse College who sang in the world-renowned Glee Club *and* played trombone in the bands? That's my youngest son, Kameron.)** Why do we almost reflexively condemn young Black boys and men based on their physical or outward appearance? If we condemn them for what they look like, or for being who they are, what role do we play in shaping who they are?

Yes, we can sit in our pristine sanctuaries and condemn our own young people, but Jesus would not have condemned them. When you tell church folks (and there's a difference between church folks and Christians) what Jesus said, they really do not want to hear it. Church folks have been wearing gold teeth long before the members

Hip Hop Is Not Our Enemy

of ThreeSixMafia were born. Church folks need to quit being so hypocritical! That is what we need to do! We are just angry with the hip-hop groups and rappers and ghetto impressarios because they can fill their mouths with real diamonds and genuine gold. We are just hating on them.

We've been sipping on E&J: that's "E" for Envy and "J" for Jealousy. When we condemn the hip-hop generation for certain things we have to take that definition all the way. What do you say you condemn them for? Calling women "hoes" and "bitches"? What if that's what the women act like? What if that's what they <u>are</u>? Let me challenge you linguistically for a moment. Let's consider what those words really mean. The word "hoe" is a derivation of the word *whore*, which is defined as "an offensive term for someone regarded as being sexually indiscriminate" (MSN Encarta Dictionary). If a person is, in fact, "sexually indiscriminate", or intentionally acting that way, what is the objection to using the term in that instance? Similarly, the word *bitch* is defined as "someone who is malicious or unpleasant" (MSN Encarta Dictionary). Again, if the shoe fits...

Not long ago, I went to see media mogul Tyler Perry's movie, "Madea's Family Reunion". At the beginning of the movie a judge forced Madea to be a foster mother to an unruly little girl. Madea did not want to do it, but she had to do it because the judge ordered her to either take care of the little girl, or go to jail. One day the little girl skipped school. When Madea confronted her about it she told Madea that the reason she did not go to school was because the other students called her names, to which Madea replied, "It don't matter what folks call you. It matters what you answer to."

That is *Madea-ology*. Yes, we can condemn our young people for doing what they do, but what is it that we are doing that is leading them to do what they do? Just because someone calls you an unflattering name does not make you that which is named.

Consider this: There are people who hear me speak at various churches and other venues who have traditional sensibilities. They object to me speaking the way that I do. I use, shall we say, colorful language. Keep in mind that I always use the language in the context of whatever text I'm speaking on at the time. Do these objectors not realize that if this kind of language is not used in proper context children will take, and use, them out of context? Do they not realize that if we teach people how such language is supposed to be used they will not fall into the trap? That is what it is. It is a trap.

Be wary when you hear church folks passing judgment on other folks. Whenever all the church folks start condemning somebody, take a step back from the situation and look at it objectively. Not long after ThreeSixMafia won their Academy Award, I appeared on a local radio station in Memphis which has a gospel music/talk format, WLOK-AM 1340, the first Black-owned radio station in Memphis. When the show's host asked me about the brouhaha surrounding whether ThreeSixMafia's members were devil worshipers, and whether they deserved the Oscar, I made the following statement: "I absolutely, categorically refuse to condemn ThreeSixMafia or any other black youth for getting out of poverty!" I refuse to condemn them! I do not really care how you get out of poverty, but baby, get out!

What ThreeSixMafia and countless other hip-hop musical artists have done is quite simple, yet profound. They have found a way to get out of poverty that bypasses formal education or training. They have found a way to use the skills, gifts, and talents they've been blessed with to escape a life of hopelessness and despair. We shouldn't begrudge them the freedom they've achieved. We should do everything we can to make sure even more of our children do the same!

Poverty is what is wrong with so many of our babies. Look at most public school systems in the United States. The systems are poor because two thirds of the children are poor. And in most large urban areas like Memphis, the overwhelming majority of those students are Black. And poverty carries with it all the attendant ills that naturally prevent poor people from achieving the heights often achieved by people of means.

At the time of this writing I serve as an elected member of the Memphis City Schools Board of Commissioners, which is the policy-making body responsible for providing every public school student a decent education in a safe learning environment. Our system made headlines recently because we opened several school-based health clinics, which are expected to be seeing the first of thousands of city school students, many already diagnosed as obese or in need of glasses, blood pressure medication and even psychiatric care.

In opening the clinics, the schools superintendent said, "We've always had the data on student health, but we haven't done anything about it." (Memphis Commercial Appeal - April 4, 2009). Schools across the nation have experimented with clinics for nearly thirty years, but there has been a resurgence in recent years because of the intractable health problems compounded and sometimes created by generational poverty in America's largest cities. Meanwhile, in those same cities, many Black Pastors seem to think that God is pleased with them sitting in their pulpits, making disparaging remarks about our children, casting aspersion on them, and condemning them to hell while the preacher drives a Cadillac!

Often we preachers wear alligator shoes and designer suits as the fruit of our ingenuity and creativity in ministering to our communities. In the minds of many church-goers, young people like ThreeSixMafia cannot get up out of poverty unless they come through the church establishment and do things the way the church says they should do them. I am not about to let church folks off the hook. Church folks have a responsibility to the young people in our neighborhoods, and we aren't discharging that responsibility by accusing them of going to hell just because they don't do the church thing. ThreeSixMafia are no more pawns of the devil than you and I are; well, I can only speak for myself on that one!

CHAPTER THREE
WHAT IS HIP-HOP ANYWAY?

What is hip-hop anyway? *We* are hip-hop. In his book entitled <u>Rap and Hip-Hop: Examining Pop Culture</u>, Jared Green defines hip-hop as "the musical medium through which the story of life in America at the end of the twentieth and beginning of the twenty-first centuries is being told." Hip-hop is a medium. A medium is a means or instrumentality for storing or communicating information. That is why we cannot escape it. Hip-hop is perpetually morphing and transforming, transmitting, responding to and shaping information about America's underbelly, her neglected step-children who are demanding that she pay attention to them, and that she do her duty to mother them, to nurture them into becoming productive citizens in a civil society.

At the same time, hip-hop, in all its inglorious hype – from video vixens to prison paternalism – is informing America of the dire consequences of continued marginalization of an entire class of people. If we don't begin to embrace the hip-hop generation we will begin to reap the antithesis of productive citizens. The antithesis of productive citizens in a civil society is a generation of *destr*uctive rebels in a society under siege. Anarchy – which is defined as, a situation in which there is a total lack of organization or control – wouldn't be far behind.

Make no mistake about it; hip-hop is here to stay. Anytime you can turn on your television and see one of hip-hop's darlings, SnoopDogg ("What's the dizzle my nizzle?") and Lee Iacocca (Mr. Establishment, the Chief Executive who led Chrysler Motor Company out of bankruptcy, the epitomy of the White Establishment) in a television commercial, riding together in a golf cart, hawking automobiles, that lets you know that hip-hop is ubiquitous, and no matter how hard you try you cannot get away from its presence and influence.

Any time you can turn on your television and see NASCAR's Dale Earnhardt, Jr. – a true representative of the traditional South if I ever saw one – and Atlanta rapper T.I. smile at each other, shake hands, exchange pleasantries, hug, and swap cars you know that hip-hop has arrived in the living room of mainstream America. Anytime a rapper like 50 Cent (aka Curtis Jackson) – whose claim to fame is based largely on the fact that he was shot nine times before his twenty-fifth birthday - can help develop his own grape-flavored vitamin water for a fledgling company, then sell his share of that company for $100 million, hip-hop and hip-hoppers have demonstrated a deft ability to negotiate the turbulent waters of the American Dream. Not to mention the fact that at the time of this writing a new movie entitled *Righteous Kill* is being promoted that stars 50 Cent and Oscar-winning actors Robert DeNiro and Al Pacino. Talk about mainstream!

If America is about anything she is about commercial success through capitalism, and hip-hop is a primary engine driving a lot of dollars into the bank accounts of countless corporations whose CEO's probably don't even listen to hip-hop music, and who would no doubt be terrified if "caught" on an elevator alone with any of hip-hop's ubiquitous ambassadors.

Why would anyone condemn Snoop, T.I., 50 Cent, or others for making millions of dollars legally? At least those hip-hoppers' children will not have to grow up in poverty. However many children they have, it'll be that many children that need not suffer for lack of money and material things. Think about it. From whose perspective is hip-hop music presented, generally? It is presented from the perspective of poor Black youngsters. It is presented from the perspective of children who live in the ghetto twenty-four hours a day, three hundred sixty-five days a year.

We cannot help it if a majority of rich white kids apparently do not have rhythm and cannot write poetry at the drop of a dime and cannot flow lyrically to an improvised beat. That is not our fault. Poverty breeds creativity. If you're reading this book you probably know what I'm talking about. If you had to, you could probably stretch a half of a potato, a quarter of an onion, and some bacon grease, and feed seven children, and have leftovers. That's creativity! It's a creativity born of struggle.

Most people I know have had to struggle to make it in life, and that struggle strengthened their character. That struggle birthed a tenacious will to do whatever is necessary to overcome obstacles. We must not frown on our own culture. Do not frown on the innate ability of our people to survive in the midst of the madness we face daily. Make up your mind right now to encourage young people wherever you encounter them. Encourage them to create whatever it is they need to create, within the limits of legality, to get up and out of poverty. And if you are a Christian, or a Muslim, or a Jew, or any of countless other faith-based belief system adherents, please resist the powerful influence of those who are so heavenly-minded that they are no earthly good.

Resist the temptation to condemn anybody and everybody who doesn't do church like you do church.

Let me revisit that radio program I participated in. Remember me saying that I was not going to condemn ThreeSixMafia for getting out of poverty? Well, shortly after I made that statement the host of the show opened up the phone lines for listener comments. There was a caller who may not have been a Black preacher, but he sure sounded like one! You can always tell, in the Black community, who the traditional preachers are. They talk a certain way. Since you may not have an audio version of this book, you'll have to use your imagination and try to *hear* this! The caller said, "Eh, Dr. Whalum, ain't ThreeSixMafia da one dat be callin' da womens B's and H's in dey music?" The caller went on to say that "dis hip-hop music makes deez children go crazy."

He said the lyrics make the young people actually do the things that the song lyrics suggest. If that were true then the three young men I'm about to introduce to you wouldn't be where they are today. James Cartwright IV, Daniel King, and Andre Thornton are young Black men who graduated from predominantly Black high schools in Memphis. Daniel and Andre graduated as Valedictorians of their respective classes, each with a grade point average well over a perfect 4.0, A. James graduated as Salutatorian of his class, coming percentage points shy of being the Valedictorian. He also had a grade point average of well in excess of 4.0 All three of these young men (in addition to being members of the same church!) absolutely love hip-hop and hip-hop music. If it is true that hip-hop music is making all young people act crazy, then James, Daniel, and Andre are aberrations. To the contrary, they are not aberrations. They are typical, gifted, motivated, loved Black men-in-the-making. And they are each attending famous colleges and universities on full scholarships!

CHAPTER FOUR

A CHALLENGE TO THE CHURCH

This is for all the Christians who are living in denial about the real world. This is for those who are so self-absorbed you don't understand that often the reason things are so bad is because we're not doing what we're empowered by God to do to make things better. This is for people who attend church on a regular basis and claim to be "saved", yet engage habitually in the kind of sinful lifestyle most preachers preach against. This is for today's equivalents of the scribes and Pharisees of Jesus' day; the ones he was referring to when he said, "Beware the leaven of the Pharisees, which is hypocrisy" (Luke 12:1, KJV).

Stop being so intellectually lazy! As a Pastor it's my job to prophetically persuade people to do better, and to collectively address society's ills and injustices. I challenge you to engage your powers of analysis in the word of God and find ways to walk out the true meaning of God's message. Start using the brain God gave you for good and not just to preserve your little piece of the pie, claiming to be "blessed and highly favored" while your community crumbles around you and your children wander aimlessly into oblivion. Stand up for our young people! How dare you keep silent when you know the great things our young people are capable of? How dare you be afraid of your own children?

The battle lines have, indeed, been drawn. This is war, but it is not war against our own children, as was declared by the Memphis Pastor I referred to in the opening chapter of this book. And speaking of Pastors, I challenge *you* too. How dare you take advantage of the spiritual authority God has given you, and subvert it to declare war on the children in your own community? I refuse to declare war on hip-hop culture. I am declaring war on the real enemies of our faith. The truth of the matter is that the devil and his imps are not paying any particular attention to hip-hop. If the devil and his imps can keep Christians from doing what Christians are empowered to do, then they don't have to be concerned about hip-hop. If the devil can keep Pastors bogged down in envy, jealousy, and ignorance he does not have to bother with ThreeSixMafia. It is a doggone shame when I literally have to have a security detail, not to protect me from gang bangers, but to protect me from these demented, drunk-on-E&J church folk!

The interesting thing is that White people (or, European-Americans, if you prefer) are adopting hip-hop culture and they are making money off of it, but we are not condemning them. Time is not long. If the devil can set it up so that the church does not welcome children off the streets then we will soon be out of business. If the devil can set it up so that the Black Pastors are shunning our own children, who will the children turn to? They are going to turn to a life of crime and end up dead or in prison. That is why the prison system is being privatized, so that they can continue to make millions and millions and millions of dollars off of our cultural dysfunction, yet we have churches on every corner.

CHAPTER FIVE

HIP-HOP IS MORE THAN MUSIC

Hip-hop is the musical medium through which the story of life in America is being told, primarily from the perspective of poor Black young people. One of the young stars of "Notorious", Sean "Puffy" Combs-produced 2009 movie about Christopher Wallace, aka hip-hop rapper Biggie Smalls, is quoted as saying, "I love hip-hop. It's a lifestyle. We all live it. You can't just listen to the music. It's bigger than music. When you wear your jeans a certain way, your swagger, it's hip-hop. Or the way you have your hat leaning. People need to know that it's more than just lyrics and rapping. It's the clothing. It's the way we eat. It's the car. It's the Gucci. It's the Ferragamo's. It's everything you live and breathe, and people need to know that." (Jamal Woolard in GIANT Magazine, December/January 2008, www.giantmag.com).

What we are really talking about is hip-hop as culture. What is culture? It is the accumulated habits, attitudes, and beliefs of a group of people that define for them their general way of life; the total set of learned activities of a people. When we talk about hip-hop culture we are not only talking about the hip-hoppers, but those of us who *react* to the hip-hoppers. So if we condemn hip-hop culture we are not just condemning the rappers and musicians and their followers, but we are condemning ourselves.

To the extent that ThreeSixMafia and others have turned to a life of whatever they have turned to; to the extent that they have done it because we have not offered them a viable option in life, then it is not their fault. It is ours. We really do not like to hear that kind of thing, do we? While we are condemning hip-hop, we have to look into the mirror and ask ourselves the question, "What have I done to correct the problems I am complaining about?"

Make no mistake, I am not defending or justifying the messages conveyed in some of our music today. I am not justifying the lyrical content of a lot of the music. There is no justification for rap lyrics like, ThreeSix's, "Tear da club up! Tear da club up! Tear da club up!" My question would be, tear da club up for *what*?! If *we* tear the club up, *we* will not *have* a club! That's just foolishness, and I would suggest to you that the hip-hop impresarios who pen such lyrics know that much of what they espouse through their songs amounts to little more than foolishness.

It is said that when someone told Biggie Smalls that some of his lyrics sounded stupid, he replied, "They sound stupid because that's what they *are*!" Yes, many of the lyrics are stupid, and are definitely not God-like, no matter how many gold crosses the rappers wear while rapping stupid lyrics. Here is a quick thumbnail measure to tell if something is of God or of the devil: if it is *de*structive it is probably of the devil; if it is *con*structive it is probably of God. It does not matter what label you put on it. If it is tearing somebody down it is of the devil. If it is building somebody up it is of God. You do not have to go to the internet, read a book, or know the artist's background. What do the lyrics make you feel like doing? How does the music make you feel? Does it tear you down or does it build you up?

You may be guilty of tearing folk down without saying a word. Any time a man would allow his own children to struggle and starve, that is tearing them down. Anytime a so-called man can have children who need clothes, shelter, counseling, and you're their daddy and you do not do anything about it, that is tearing them down.

I am not justifying song lyrics like, "Let's start a riot!" For what reason would we want to start a riot, especially when there is no one in here but us? It makes no sense. Here's another real example from a rap song by St. Louis rapper, Nelly: "Rob a jewelry store and tell 'em, 'make me a grill'." First of all, most of your teeth are so bad you need a partial more than you need a grill. You need some root canal work. You need some fillings. You do not need a grill. You are going to mess around and put a grill on those teeth and all of them are going to fall out. You do not need a grill, man. You need a drill!

My point is that some of the hip-hop rap lyrics are indefensible. One cannot defend them, so that is not what I am trying to do, but hip-hop culture does not have a monopoly on indefensible lyrics. How about a couple of examples from back in the day? Remember "Me and Mrs. Jones"?

> *Me and Mrs. Jones -*
> *we've got a thing going on.*
> *We both know that it's wrong,*
> *but it's much too strong*
> *to let it go now.*

How can we jump on ThreeSixMafia for telling us it's hard out here for a pimp, when Billy Paul is actively promoting adultery? Did we condemn Billy Paul? Did we tell our church congregations to go home and burn their eight-track tapes? And what about this one; "If Loving You Is Wrong, I Don't Want To Be Right" You remember! Luther Ingram sang it:

> *"Your friends tell you it's no future in loving a married man.*
> *If I can't see you when I want, I'll see you when I can.*
> *If loving you is wrong, I don't want to be right!"*

I don't remember hearing or reading about local Pastors preaching fire and brimstone sermons about the apocalyptic designs of STAX records and soul music! Let's stop being so small-minded. They're just songs, man!

CHAPTER SIX

WE COMPARTMENTALIZE ALL THE TIME

After ThreeSixMafia won their Oscar a local newspaper columnist who happens to be Black and Christian wrote a lengthy opinion piece chastising the group for their style of music, including the winning song lyrics. I interviewed her for a local radio station one day, and asked if she thought she could separate the group's significant industry achievement of winning an Academy Award from her disdain for the objectionable lyrics in much of their music, and give them their props for bringing another Academy Award home to Memphis. (They weren't the first, because STAX legend Isaac Hayes won in the same category in 1971 for the movie soundtrack to "Shaft"). She said she couldn't do it. She felt that she couldn't, in good conscience, recognize their significant accomplishment while still objecting to what she felt was bad content. It was too much of a double standard, she thought.

I disagreed with her then, and I disagree with her now. The reason I disagree with her is that we observe double standards all the time! It is just that we do it in judging ourselves and not so much when it comes to judging others. It's called compartmentalization. We compartmentalize all the time. To compartmentalize means to separate into detached compartments, divisions, or categories. You mean to tell me you cannot congratulate me for winning an Oscar because I have a song that says something ugly? Come on now. It is impossible? Now would be a good time to look in the mirror. Why is it so easy for us to give ourselves the benefit of the doubt, and so hard to give that same benefit to others? If we are going to condemn folks let us condemn everybody that needs to be condemned. That is where it gets uncomfortable. We have to start checking ourselves then. Are we doing everything we are supposed to be doing?

It may surprise some to know that we're not fooling anybody with our "holier-than-thou" façade. Hip-hop aficionados understand our duplicitous and self-serving belly-aching. The following is an open letter "to the government" from Mississippi-born, award-winning, best-selling rapper, David Banner.

A Letter To The Government: Stop Attacking The Kids

To all the black 'so called leaders'. Al, Oprah, Jesse, etc. etc, etc, etc...I'm saddened by your current direction and current 'pet projects' you guys have taken under your wing at the expense of Young Black America. As an urban professional living in this crazy world, I dare ask, who are you leading? I listen to what you say, I hear you complain about the youth, and about the direction of our lives, the kids, and where Black America is going and yet I still ask-who are you guys leading? And most importantly, where are we going?

Do we know the goal we are trying to reach before we get there? Have we identified our end before articulating our means to an end! Who are you REALLY reaching? Why do you feel the need to attack the young generation for the things we are doing? "WHO DID WE LEARN THESE THINGS FROM? We are trying to have fun in the midst of our traumatic circumstances. People are trying to make a living by any means necessary, people are voicing their experiences, people are speaking the truth about situations and honestly the truth hurts and sometimes it's ugly.

If music/hip-hop/ rappers are wrong with the language they use, the images they portray in their videos-then come talk to us-I use the term 'us' as a collective because I'm defending what I have a passion for so this also involves me. Pull us to the side and say "hey kids, that's not the way to go" and then we can say "change what we see daily so we can sing and rap about the roses and not about the bullets". We will say, "Help give us better situations to create better verbal material." Don't just go running off to the media to air the dirty laundry of the family and not expect us to fight back in some kind of way. What you are doing is wrong and it's pissing off a lot of people with less money and camera time!

Young Black America's problem is not Hip-Hop or the music, young Black America's problem is Old White America. In the young black community, there is a growing level of resentment toward the 'so called leaders' because you guys DON'T WANT TO REALLY FIX OUR PROBLEMS. You guys don't really want to be on our side fighting for better school systems, more after school programs, more money for college funding!

Where are you leaders at when there's a need to break down to the freshman in college on how not to get caught up with credit cards by signing up for an MBNA card, with high interest rates that eventually screw up your credit and makes it that much harder for you to become a homeowner after you graduate college pending you can find a job in your field after you've spent all this money in student loans! Where are those seminars? Dubois had it right when he spoke of the Talented Tenth! Rally around us to help teach us about THIS life! It's not our fault that the world is messed up and filled with debauchery. It's not our fault that our communities are screwed!

The problems in our community should not fall in our lap. And if you begin to hold us accountable for simply our words-then I will begin to hold you accountable for your actions; or lack thereof. Right is right and wrong is wrong. You as our leaders should have taken a better approach to gaining the attention of those that you are dissatisfied with and had a conversation with them. You don't scold your child in public without fair warning!

Al Sharpton: You run around towns and cities speaking words of wanting to better our community by cleaning up the airwaves. You hold rallies in front of radio stations saying turn off the music and clean the airwaves. You want to shutdown local stations that are playing urban music when most of these local stations house and employ the same people in your community-the black community. When you visit any station in any city (big or small) playing urban/rap music, the staff is generally black. Now if those stations were to ever shut down-where do those employees go?

Al, if you are for the people, where was your rally when the 3 college students were executed in New Jersey by black men? Where is the rally at for those families and that neighborhood??? I don't see you out there asking for justice yet that incident happened in a black community. If someone was to rap about "how f***** up black on black crime is and how even if you go to college you aren't safe on the streets and nigga's aint' s----"-that kind of tone is offensive to you and you want to stop that! If that's the truth, then why are you censoring it? No, you need to stop the crime before it happens so that there is no gangster song about a gangster situation.

Oprah: you recently held you a town hall meeting dedicating 2 days of talk to have an open forum about the "Nappy Headed Ho" comment from Imus. Everyone had their 2 cents to say and yet the people that needed to REALLY be there were not at all on your panel of 'experts'. The questions all were about "why use the word ho or b**** or nigga etc." yet the rappers

Hip Hop Is Not Our Enemy

in question ala Nelly, Snoop, Ludacris weren't anywhere present on your panel. In my eyes you had all the wrong people on there representing and speaking on behalf of other people. Common is great but he's not a gangsta. If you had a problem with the true content of rap songs then where were those that do that kind of rap 100%?

Oprah, you want to talk about change, and about having us not call women in rap songs "bitches" and "hoes" but one thing I noted, you had all men on your panel of executives. Russell is wonderful but he's not the Zenith when it comes to new school rappers or their new school mentality. Kevin Liles is great but what happened to Sylvia Rhone the head of the label that Nelly is signed to, or Kathy Hughes the head of Radio One or Deborah Lee the head of BET. If the problem really was about women and the "bitch, ho" term being used, where were those ladies to speak on their stance on this issue? They are the ones with the ultimate say pulling all the strings and yet they weren't duly noted as absent from your panel!

Oprah you are supposed to protect us, I can find more harm being done to the black community by the movies and sponsors you promote than any rap song. Just like your son or daughter, niece or nephew…rappers are just kids growing into their own. They aren't always right, but they aren't always wrong either. If our path is misguided, then help us get back on the right road. I'm young, I'm black, and I'm a hard worker. I'm from the hood where mothers leave their kids in the hands of strangers and never look back, I've been with killers, dope dealers, b******, church folk, grandparents, bad parenting from good parents, pushers, junkies, robbers, middleclass workers, but that's the life I've been around. <u>Gunshots and church hymns usually go hand in hand in most neighborhoods.</u> *(Author's emphasis).*

The grim reality for a lot of kids out there living alone is that life is harsh and cold; kids grow up faster than they want to because they are forced to! Kids are growing up in situations that are f***** up. So the songs we listen to mirror the things we see, the things we dream about and the fantasies

Dr. Kenneth T. Whalum, Jr.

we have! Don't change the songs I listen to, change the circumstance from which it comes from---then the situation will be better! Growing up in this world of hip-hop it's disheartening to see our 'so called leaders' leave us out to dry.

Fine you don't like what we say. Fine disagree with our choice of topics; however, the things we talk about aren't new. We didn't invent the term pimps, pushers, hoes, tricks, doobies, nigga's and gansta's. Hip-hop didn't create that. Those words were left here for us to use by you guys, your generation. This life we are continuing to live was handed to us by the people before us who didn't do much to clean it up. There may never be a time that we agree on anything, but there is always room for change. As a family-we will agree to disagree but it's the synergy in which we do it. If you are on one extreme tangent, and I'm on another, we will never meet eye to eye. At the same time, I will not allow you to bash, yell, condemn, and have a condescending tone on my source of refuge and happiness.

As you leaders call out the hip-hop community saying that we are wrong for what we do and how we do it, I am CALLING EACH OF YOU OUT saying you are wrong for what you are doing to us. How dare you guys not call Nelly, Snoop, Lil Wayne, David Banner, Jim Jones, Akon, Rick Ross, Fabulous, 50 Cent, Young Buck, Bun B, Too Short and say lets talk this through. Do you even know who ANY of these people are??????? You are so disconnected from us that we don't even look at you for guidance. If you really want to change something, start by changing your dialogue. Don't talk at us, talk to us! –DAVID BANNER

***

Now, David Banner, why don't you say what you <u>really</u> mean? I think the Church needs to give Mr. Banner's words serious consideration. I agree with him wholeheartedly, and deep down inside you know he's telling the truth, don't you?

CHAPTER SEVEN

DON'T LET THE DEVIL WIN!

Essentially, here's the deal: the devil thinks that he has an opportunity now to destroy the work we have done as the body of Christ. We have done great things. If it was not for the body of Christ, the church universal, I believe God would have destroyed this world a long time ago. And even though I agree with David Banner's assessment of the realities of the church's deafening silence about the condition of our streets, I think he would agree with me when I say that if it weren't for the church – especially the Black church – The United States of America would still be operating under Jim Crow government. Don't forget, it was preachers and Pastors, Black and White, who did the grunt work of demonstrations and demanding change.

Any catalogue of effective civil rights leaders in the 1950's and 1960's is replete with the names of Black preachers like Dr. King. Even then, of course, Dr. King's most insidious opposition came from within those same ecclesiastical ranks. Little has changed in that regard. If the devil can cause us to attack each other then we have no hope.

Matthew 11:19 says, "The Son of man came eating and drinking and they say, Look, a glutton and a winebibber, a friend of tax collectors and sinners." The truth of the matter is that if Jesus was reincarnated in the flesh today, the same folk who are condemning hip-hop would condemn Jesus. Look at the kind of a person he was. Jesus did not come through here talking with a dialect typical of a southern Black preacher. He did not come here trying to pretend that he had achieved a level of perfection and that he did not ever associate with "those people" any more. He didn't disassociate himself from his culture's equivalent of today's gang bangers, players, pimps, hustlers, thugs, prostitutes, and strippers. He didn't act as if he was better than them. He didn't hang out only with the *highfaulutin'* church folks of his day, the scribes and Pharisees.

According to the verse, Jesus came eating and drinking, and hanging out with sinners. The word *gluttonous* in this text does not just mean eating to live, but living to eat. Have you ever known a person who, whenever there is any food anywhere, something happens to them? They lose all their cool points. They go crazy. They start acting as if they're starving to death. That's a glutton. Jesus called himself a glutton. That means a voracious eater. That means eating like a buzzard to road-kill; like a dog to some raw meat; like a lion on the Serengeti trail devouring a gazelle. That is the kind of person Jesus described himself as.

Some people with traditional sensibilities might have a problem with me describing Jesus in the words that he used to describe himself. If your church has you that chicken, if your church upbringing has you gun shy and nervous about hearing the truth, you ought to hurry up and leave it. Jesus said they called him a glutton. They would not have called him that if they had not seen them hanging out with other gluttons.

Look what else he called himself, a winebibber. That is just another word for "drunk" or "wino". Some of you ladies who are hard on your men for drinking, ease up for a minute. If he is a drinker I understand if you are upset, but if you are, let's say, an overeater you are basically no better than he is. He passed out because he had too much to drink, and you passed out because you ate six chickens and twelve biscuits!

Consider the Amplified Version of that same verse, Matthew 11:19: "The Son of man came eating and drinking with others, and they said behold, a glutton and a wino, a friend of tax collectors and especially wicked sinners." If Jesus was a friend of *especially* wicked sinners it's probably safe to say he would befriend today's hip-hop adherents.

God says that the people who need to receive what they read in this book are going to get it. Notice what I said. God said that the people who need to receive what they read in this book will get it. That indicates that there are some who won't get it, but that's okay. Never before have we as the body of Christ been given approval by God to move into some of the areas that we are about to move into. Some of the specific things that God is going to have us doing in our local churches, I really have no idea what they are.

One thing I am certain of is as we gather weekly (those of us who are faithful) the Holy Spirit will reveal to us sometimes as a unit, sometimes the Lord will speak through the Pastor or through somebody else specifically what it is we are supposed to do. At other times the Holy Spirit will speak to you individually inside of your spirit, inside of your soul, inside of your mind specific instructions that you are to carry out as we move forward under this military anointing that God has placed on our lives.

The reason I have been (I am always straight, uncut, no chaser) almost caustic at times, almost to the point of being unbearable, almost to the point of being like a really, really mean drill sergeant, almost to the point of being like somebody who is trying to make you do something you are not capable of doing, is when you have been given the kind of responsibility that God has given us as a body we do not have time to coddle people. If you notice the people who are needy have been needy. Think about the people in your church who have been needy. How long have they been needy? They have been needy since you have known them. If it is not one thing it is another.

The anointing that we have calls upon us to minimize contact with those who would draw us away from the more weighty matters, the dangerous matters that God has for us to carry out in this world today. The reason some of you have fallen out with people that you used to be close to in church is not because you have something against them or that they have something against you. It is that it was time for there to be a separation. I am not saying you are not friends anymore, but I am saying you are not riding in the same car anymore. It is sort of like these motorcycles with a sidecar. The motorcycle cannot go as fast as it can go because it has to be concerned about the sidecar.

Some of you are drivers and some of you are riders. We need drivers and riders, but there comes a time when there has to be some advance work done. There has to be some reconnoitering. That is a military term and it means that sometimes some folk have got to go behind the enemy lines and do some spying. They have got to behind enemy lines, blend in with the enemy, and gather information, not to use while you are gathering it, but to bring it back to the camp and feed it to the general, so that the general can process it with the commander-in-chief, and then devise a strategy. What we are talking about is warfare.

Do you have children? Do you agree that it is time to reclaim our children? We cannot reclaim them if we do not know what the enemy has planned for them. We cannot know what the enemy has planned if we never want to hear anything out there, we never want to be bothered

Hip Hop Is Not Our Enemy

with anybody out there. If you got what you got from God you do not have to worry about the enemy rubbing off on you. The enemy has to worry about you rubbing off on him! As we come to the close of a phase in the history of the body of Christ we are getting ready to come to more significant military maneuvers.

Just consider, are we really here to transform lives, empower people, and release an army? Churches that are having church every week, what are they doing? I do not know. What is the typical church doing right now in terms of military assignments? I do not know. You work with them every day on your job. What are they doing? What are they talking about? The members of my congregation have friends and relatives in those traditional churches, and they tell me they are talking about church as usual, building churches, what God can do for them personally, having fish fries. They are talking about how much they shouted on Sunday and had a good time, but then they come out doing the same crazy stuff. Some are talking about sewing seeds into their ministry because they are starting a new church. A lot of people are talking about current events: everything negative that is happening in the news, whether it is political or the daily murders in Memphis. Some are talking about how many big-time gospel entertainers they can bring into their church.

Please do not misunderstand me. I am not casting negative light on what they are saying. I am not judging what they are talking about. I am sharing with you what my congregation tells me people from traditional churches are talking about. They are talking about how wicked the world is, not being in it, and not being engaged with changing it. That is what they are talking about, doing nothing. They are talking about the ministry they do within the community, but they are not adding anybody to the mix of members in their local churches. One of my congregants tells me, "I work in the school so they are talking about how bad these kids are and how we cannot do anything with these kids and 'these kids and these kids.'"

They are talking about each other. They are talking about getting new members. Another of my congregants who works in the school system, hears them talking about how they are not bringing the world into their church and how proud they are of that. This is an example of what I mean by saying that if being in Christ is not allowing us to have an impact in the world what good is it? If members of local church bodies are talking about things like this, if they are talking about how proud they are to maintain the purity of their tradition and they are not "letting this mess" up in their church, the rap and all that stuff, what do you think about that in light of what Jesus is saying in this text I have discussed thus far? It would be different if this were written by somebody other than Jesus, if someone other than Jesus were speaking.

It is time to apply the information we have received through our readings of sacred scripture to our everyday work. It is time to quit playing church and get about our business. Stop playing; put up or shut up. We need to embrace our children, not just the ones we birthed but our community of children. Go back to the neighborhoods where you grew up, embrace them, and give them purpose and a meaning. Stop judging other people and look at what you are doing in the eyes of God. I think God is saying, "I have given you the power. I have brought the word to you that you need to go and take back the city, take back the children, get up off yourselves and do it."

We have no more excuses for not doing what we know is the right thing to do. We have to get up off our butts and go out there to the other people, the same kind of people that are talked about in this Bible, and show them another way. It is time for us to act with courage regardless of whatever the cost is. It is time to speak up instead of being quiet. It is time to act instead of being passive, to stop talking about

Hip Hop Is Not Our Enemy

our children and start talking with them, to develop and implement - actively implement - a strategic plan that will get our youth back involved, save them from what is going on, and save us.

God wants you to set aside self and to do what He wants you to do and it may not be pleasant. It may not be what you want to do, but it is what He has called you to do. We as a people, God's people – Black, White and Brown - have to be receptive to all people and we have a spiritual responsibility to mobilize the lost and stop judging people. Stop talking about it and be about it! We cannot expect any better behavior from the communities, from our children, if we do not show them any better behavior. So it is our responsibility to start showing better behavior. We do not need to talk if we are not going to do anything about what is wrong in our community.

You know, we cannot sit back and wait for somebody else to step up. God has given every person something to offer other people and we have to reach inside of ourselves and find out what it is that God has given us and not sit back and just wait. Go ahead and step forward and do what you have to do. We need to stop saying that our children do not have anything to say to us. Let them speak up. If you are not going to get busy, hit the door. Let the door knob hit you where the good Lord split you! We are always judging our children as though they do not have anything to say. Children have a lot to say because they are catching a lot of hell at school and everywhere else, so we need to stop and listen to them.

The point is to stop being so judgmental. If you look at ThreeSixMafia or similar groups, you would think because of the way they dress and because of the fact that their music is so aggressive, so violent, that their character can be described in the same way. After seeing the interview I did with them and seeing that they have such a foundation in God, it just makes you think that you cannot really judge people based on their outside package or appearance. You have to really focus on what is within and how people carry themselves. Church, we have a responsibility to shoulder.

We cannot just sit back and allow everybody else to do the work needed to make progress in our communities. I think that it is our responsibility, from the youngest person to the oldest person, to mobilize as an army against the enemy because if an army has one weak person then they cannot win the battle. The battle is going to be lost. The army is going to lose because they will have a weak link in the army and that will allow some person from the enemy's army to get inside your lines and beat you. So everybody has to play a part in the warfare against Satan and his minions, imps and things of that nature.

One child in my congregation recounted an experience she had with envious and jealous classmates: "All year at my school these girls are mad at me because I am a straight-A student... my mom and my dad told them to leave me alone and stop bothering me and...the leader, who is a girl, got her cousin, who is a boy, to try to jump on me. I guess he thought I was going to back down. When I tried to hit him I tore my rotator cuff." This child is a straight "A" student and because of E&J she ended up with an injury and somebody is going to have to pay for the treatment. We, as Christians, are empowered to do something to come against envy and jealousy among our children. What are we going to do?

CHAPTER EIGHT
WE DON'T HAVE MUCH TIME

We do not have a lot of time, and we have quite a bit we have to do before Jesus comes back. Hip-hop culture is not our enemy. People with traditional sensibilities really believe that hip-hop culture and young people are our enemies. That is why they are afraid to come out of their homes at night. I have actually heard Pastors in our community say that the reason they had to stop holding night worship services is because it has gotten so "bad", and the people "won't come out". We're so intimidated as a people that we are afraid to say what needs to be said.

Many of us seem to believe that our own children are our enemies, but our children are not our enemies. Hip-hop is a musical medium through which the story of life in America is being told, typically from the perspective of poor, black, inner-city young people. They are giving expression to their experience. Their experience is a part of our experience. Our experience is a part of their experience. We cannot save them if we continually attack them. We cannot save them if we make them feel like they are the devil's pawns, and that they are no good because of who they are. Who they are is a function of who we are.

We are living at a critical juncture in the history of humankind, not just the history of America, specifically Black America. The crime that we are seeing is a function of hip-hop culture. Gang banging is a function of hip-hop culture. If you look at the popular hip-hop musical artists and then look at the typical gang banger, you cannot tell the difference between them, based on their appearance. If our experience in church does not sanctify us to the point where we can make a real difference out here on these streets then our experience at church is a doggone waste of time.

If my Christianity doesn't activate my spirituality to change my reality, then my Christianity is no good. What good is my Christianity if I can't use my spirituality to change my reality? There is a lot to say. A lot of it is in the news recently. I just do not think we can condemn our own young people and expect to have them make a positive difference in their world and respond to us in a positive way. You might not agree with that. If not, you need to go to a church where they believe that you can say one thing and do another. You need to be at a church where the Pastor talks the talk, but has a girlfriend on every side of the church. And you might want to put this book down now, because in the words of the Grammy-winning Dixie Chicks, "I'm not ready to make nice. I'm not ready to back down" to man's vain religious tradition. Sin is sin. It does not matter who commits it.

CHAPTER NINE
NOT READY TO MAKE NICE

Obviously, what we think about our young people who are enmeshed in the hip-hop lifestyle is not making much of a difference in their minds anyway. Evidently, who we think God is, and our philosophy about God are not preventing hip-hoppers from claiming God for themselves, despite our protestations about their unworthiness. Apparently, their philosophy runs along this line: "Just because you do not like my gold teeth, my sagging, baggy pants, and my raunchy lyrics does not make me what you say I am. Your opinion of me does not define me. Your self-righteous condemnation of my creativity cannot stop me from believing in God for myself."

ThreeSixMafia's Juicy J, whose given name is Jordan Houston, is from North Memphis, a section of Memphis known for decaying homes and shuttered store fronts. In a JET Magazine interview Mr. Houston was asked what it meant for hip-hop that ThreeSixMafia was nominated for and received an Academy Award. In response he said, "Hip-hop is taking over." I imagine that statement makes some people in the Black church community nervous. But it shouldn't make you nervous unless you do not understand that you are hip-hop too.

Houston was also asked, "What do you say about these folk who think that because you write controversial lyrics, saying that you are a pimp, what do you say about these people who say you are sending a bad message?" To which he matter-of-factly replied, "I'm going to pray for them." Jordan Houston, aka Juicy J, the one with the menacing aura, said that he's going to pray for the very ones who accused him of being a pawn of the devil. That's deep, isn't it? Church folks are the ones hating on Juicy J and ThreeSixMafia, calling them "pawns of the devil" and "enemies of God". But here's the pawn saying, "I'm going to pray for them."

Some church folk don't pray *period*, let alone pray for other people. They would rather point their collective finger and look down their noses at the masses. Church folks talk about other church folks. Rarely do they pray for them. There are a lot of things I do not know, but I grew up in church. I've been in church literally all my life, and I know church folks. You probably do too. The reason a lot of people stop going to church in the first place is because of church folks. Most of us PK's (preachers' kids) learned how to be *slick* at church.

The first time I kissed a girl in the mouth was in the stairwell at church. The Pastor's son can get away with a whole lot of stuff, you know. I know church folk, and I was not in church trouble by myself. I did not kiss myself. She was ready, willing, and able. I am not talking about a peck on the cheek, either. I am talking about lip-locking and tongue-plunging. It was in church. Church folk are nothing nice. Sometimes the very ones sitting up in church on Sunday morning looking holy and righteous are cursing somebody under their breath at the same time. And the funny thing is, this behavior stays with a person throughout their church experience, from an early age to a late one. It is as if we perfect the art of being fake.

CHAPTER TEN

FAKE-PHONY-BOLONEY-PSEUDO-SEMI-SAINTS

Phony: a hypocrite; a person who professes beliefs and opinions that he or she does not hold, in order to conceal his or her real feelings or motives. Juicy J said he would pray for the church folks who condemned him for winning an Oscar. These same church folks profess to believe in a merciful and forgiving and longsuffering God. Really? Consider this: The Memphis Music Commission and the City of Memphis honored ThreeSixMafia for their landmark artistic achievement. But some over-zealous Pastors were raising hell about ThreeSixMafia.

ThreeSixMafia got a key to the city while over-zealous Pastors and other assorted church folks were denouncing them. Jordan Houston, Juicy J, was asked on another occasion, "What does it mean to you that you, a group from Memphis, received an Academy Award, keys to the city, and a plaque in the Rock-n-Roll Hall of Fame?" He said, "It is a blessing." Church folks would have said, "I want to thank my mama" after engaging in the following hyperbole, "First giving honor to God who is the head of my life…"

We cannot have church in a vacuum. We cannot have church and ignore what is going on around us in the streets. We have got to make a difference! In the United States of America, if you are Black, young, and poor, and another hurricane comes ashore, you are going to be on top of Dixie Homes (a public housing complex in Memphis) just like they were in the ninth ward of New Orleans. You are going to be on top of Dixie Homes saying, "Hey! Save me!" The same camera man that is filming the church folk talking about ThreeSixMafia will be filming you drowning, but you go to church every Sunday.

Once your children get of age they are not paying attention to the church because the church has never done anything of substance for them. It is about getting out of poverty. If we cannot get our children out of poverty we are of all men most miserable. Teachers and school administrators know good and well you cannot reach the mind of a poor, hungry child without addressing their very real, very immediate, very basic needs. We have to make a difference, and if Christ in us cannot give us what we need to begin to grapple with the issues we deal with on a daily basis then Christ is not worth having. I said it!

If we condemn all of hip-hop, then our children will not even have a creative outlet. They will not be able to create and do those things that they need to do to express themselves, because hip-hop is a musical medium through which the story of life in America is told. It is the lyrics of the songs that are objectionable, not the creative process through which the song came into being.

We have our own hip-hop rap group right in our church. If we condemn hip-hop then it would not be possible to encourage their creative expression. Our young people do not look any different than

ThreeSixMafia. They are the creative forces that keep coming up with these original beats and rhymes, but the lyrics are sanctified. What if I was like most traditional Pastors who tell our children to "get that mess out of the church"? I've actually heard Pastors say that! Just thinking about it makes me want to cuss real bad!

Our children are literally dying in the streets. If we condemn the culture, we condemn the children. Allow me to address those of you with traditional sensibilities: what you have to do is open up your mind and heart and stop being so scary. You know these young people are catching flak. You know the devil wants them on his side. You know the devil wants them to write lyrics that are not glorifying God. The devil has latched on to the fact that they are creative and talented. He wants to appropriate their skills for his cause.

Rather than talking about them, berating them, and condemning them you need to be praying for them because the power that works in them is greater than the power that works in the world. I firmly believe that. Don't you?

CHAPTER ELEVEN

SHAKE THAT LAFFY TAFFY

As I said earlier, evidently the negative remarks we make about hip-hoppers do not keep them from believing in God. Are you familiar with the song, "Laffy Taffy"? You should be. "Laffy Taffy" is a song by a group called D4L, also known as Down 4 Life. The front man is named Mooky B. In still another JET Magazine article, Mooky was asked, "You said that D4L is a movement. Why do you say that?" He replied, "We all come from different projects." Mookie was not talking about an extra credit assignment in Science class when he said refers to "projects". He was talking about the ghetto.

In his case, he was talking about public housing. Reader, please tell me you have not been living in the suburbs so long that you have forgotten what the projects are! Mookie B said, "We are all from different projects, not to mention that the different projects cannot get along. How fly is it that we took a major negative and turned it into a positive? How many people can say they got warring projects to come together and do something positive? People that would normally not speak to each other unless it was to throw disrespect are, through music, showing each other love." Church folks (remember, there's a difference between church folks and Christians!) know very little about showing each other real love. Church folks are too busy condemning our own young people, saying they are the pawns of the devil, to show love. Sounds to me like Mooky B is talking about the transformative power of love, even though he probably wouldn't call it that.

JET Magazine also asked Mooky B, "Did you think 'Laffy Taffy' would be the song that would give you national recognition?" Listen to what Mooky B said: "Yeah, we thought it because *we knew God had something big planned for us.*" What are church folks going to do with this kind of stuff? Mooky goes on to say, "He (God) led; we followed… We just need to be patient. Quick and easy ain't always the best way to get where you want to be." I don't know, but it sounds like Mooky B might have been reading in the Bible where it says that "the race is not given to the swift, nor to the strong, but to the one that endures until the end"! (I'm paraphrasing, of course.)

Mooky B is one of the same ones that church folks condemn, even though his words contain this kind of wisdom. I know a whole bunch of church ladies who if they had not been in such a hurry to get a husband they would not have had any children, but they are condemning the young folk. All they had to do is talk to Mooky B. I have known some church women who were quick and easy. Finally, JET said to Mooky B, "Some may look at 'Laffy Taffy' as a one-hit wonder. It is not your average song on the radio and fans can be fickle to say the least." Mooky B said, "Since we put God first we are not even worried about that one-hit wonder junk." If church folks would just learn how to put God first! They asked, "Mooky, why did you name it 'Laffy Taffy'?" Mooky B said, "We wanted to put out something sweet for the ladies. There are already enough songs calling them bitches and hoes. We wanted to give them something different, something they could dance to; plus who does not like something sweet every once in a while?"

I know you may be tired of reading about Mooky B by now, but hang with me for one more point. When asked if he labeled himself as a hip-hop artist, Mooky said, "Hip-hop is a way of life and expression, and you should be able to express yourself however you want to." Mooky, I couldn't have said it better myself! Reader, can I get an AMEN?

CHAPTER TWELVE

ESPECIALLY WICKED SINNERS HAVE WISDOM TOO

"The Son of man came eating and drinking with others, and they said behold, a glutton and a wino, a friend of tax collectors and especially wicked sinners."-Matthew 11:19

We are living in some critical times. This text was taken from a time that is similar to the times we live in now. Everything was in upheaval. Stuff was getting turned topsy-turvy. The government was tripping. The church was tripping. Jesus was just doing his thing. He was teaching, preaching, and healing. There was a man named John the Baptist who had been arrested. He heard of the things Jesus was doing and sent two of his own disciples to check Jesus out. He had his own clique he was representing too, you know. Everybody who has anything to offer has a clique. If you have anything going for you or if you have any charisma at all you have a clique. You have a circle of influence.

The principles I am lifting now are universal principles. These principles are not exclusively Christian principles. If you have anything going for you somebody is going to follow you. John sent two members of his clique to check Jesus out. John sent two disciples. He told them to ask Jesus, "Are you the one that is coming or do we look for another one?" Jesus said, "Go back and tell them what you see." In other words, quit all the talking. I am so sick of people talking. Let me *see* something. He said, "Go back and tell your people what you see: the blind receive their sight, the dead are raised, the lame walk, the deaf are speaking now, demons are being cast out. Tell them what you *see*."

Jesus said to John, "What did you go out into the wilderness to *see*? Did you go out to *see* a man with soft clothing on?" In other words, what are you looking for in a spiritual leader? Are you looking for somebody who wears spiritual looking clothes and speaks with an erudite tonal inflections and uses the word "Doc" when referring to other preachers? (If you're Black and Southern, you definitely get this!)

Jesus said that folks with soft clothes are in the king's house, but John came eating wild honey and locusts and hair all matted up with what probably looked like dreadlocks. Wake up, church folk! Wake up! Just because the preacher dresses in a custom-made Italian-style suit does not mean that he is any closer to God than Bob Marley-n-them. John the Baptist probably had dreads because he did not care how he looked. Now here he is with dreads in his head. He is wearing animal fur, but he was not a glutton and did not drink alcohol and they still found something wrong with him.

Church folks are always going to find fault in somebody they do not understand. The truth of the matter is that if you are confident in who you are, then what somebody else says or thinks will not threaten you. He, the Son of Man, said, "I come eating and drinking and I did not do it by myself." Did you know that some Catholics and Episcopalians drink a lot of wine? In fact, I know some people who converted to Catholicism because they drink wine openly.

In the traditional church, especially the Black Baptist church, they have what they call, "The Church Covenant". Church folk enter into this covenant. They give "The Church Covenant" more credence than the Ten Commandments, and they put huge copies up on the wall in their sanctuaries. They tell a lot of lies in there. They say they are not going to drink any alcohol whatsoever. They would not have liked Jesus. They would have kicked him out of the church.

Listen to what Jesus says. He says, "wisdom is justified and vindicated by what she does and by her children." You cannot be worried about what folks say about you. A lot of church folk do not have wisdom. That is why I want to say this. Here is the definition of the word wisdom as Jesus used it: "broad and full of intelligence; used of the knowledge of very diverse matters." Just because you walk around telling people you are Holy Ghost-filled, and saying you're blessed and highly favored does not mean you have wisdom. If I ask you how you are doing then just tell me how you are doing. I will know that you are blessed and highly favored because you are using your blessing to bless somebody else. Just go on about your business.

Wisdom is full of intelligence. Wisdom is varied knowledge on things human and divine acquired by acuteness and experience. "Varied knowledge" means you know about a lot of stuff. Do not be so small-minded that you know nothing about anything. You need some real-world experience beyond your street address and zip code. It is easy to slip into a spiritual trance when your experience is so limited. Then you start turning your focus on yourself. Then you become super-spiritual and then nobody can do anything with you. You are walking on air now. Your house is falling down around you, but you can tell me a revelation about myself. You are on the brink of bankruptcy, but you have a word from God for me. Creditors are calling your house, you have an unlisted number, but you have a revelation from God for me. You have nothing for me! Your marriage is in shambles, but you are going to give me a word of wisdom. I have a word for *you*: **Hush**!

According to Jesus, wisdom is justified by what she does. She is justified by her children. I do not care how holy you sit up and look. If you have wisdom your lifestyle will reflect it in every area. Quit letting these church folks run you ragged. They will drive you crazy. You take advice from folk who are riding on fumes right now, but they are going to tell you how to prosper. When you have true wisdom you have spiritual insight. You understand things. God reveals things to you. That is wisdom.

What Jesus is talking about has nothing to do with the clothes you have on, whether or not you have gold in your mouth, or whether or not you write rhymes. What is wisdom? Wisdom is skill in the management of your affairs. You cannot manage your way out of a wet paper bag, but you are having discussions with folk about spiritual matters. You cannot even control your own household. Your husband does not even take you seriously because you are a fool. Your wife ignores you routinely because you have no sense, but you are going to advise folk in deep spiritual matters.

Meanwhile these children are out here dying while you are playing church. Wisdom is also defined as devout and proper prudence in intercourse. I did not say *sexual* intercourse, which is what so many of our people are experts in. Wisdom is *intellectual* intercourse, which is conversation.

Did you know there is an art to conversation? If we could raise these babies up and simply teach them how to introduce themselves, if we could teach a boy just simply how to shake hands, that would be good. When someone extends their hand to you they do not want a dap. They want you to grasp their hand firmly. You look them in their eyes and you say something very simple: "Hello; my name is Kenneth T. Whalum, Jr. It's nice to meet you." Trust me, "Whattup, dog?" does not lend itself to the art of conversation. A firm handshake will get you farther than a fake resume' will.

Let's say you approach somebody for employment. You don't have much in the way of experience or education, but you have dignity about yourself. You go up to somebody and you say, "Hello, My name is_____ and it is a pleasure to meet you." I guarantee you something in their mind takes notice. Consider the following slice of my own personal history:

The night of the election when I ran against Bob Patterson for Shelby County Trustee, and lost to him, the LORD gave me wisdom. I went on television and spoke very highly of my opponent. I went to his victory party. My wife, my little babies, and I went. We walked in. I found him and walked up to him, standing up straight and tall, and I said, "How are you doing, Mr. Patterson? I want you to know I congratulate you on a race well run." The next day he called me and offered me a position and not just any position, a management position making good money. It is because even though I lost, I am not a loser.

Wisdom says that you need to learn how to interact with other folks who might not be like you. Wisdom is devout and proper prudence in intercourse with men who are not disciples of Christ. Wisdom does not condemn hip-hop, no matter how misguided some of their iconic representatives might seem to be. Wisdom says, "Congratulations ThreeSixMafia, on doing what you do. Congratulations on the influence you have on these children. Congratulations on selling millions of CD's. Congratulations on getting out of poverty so that your children do not have to grow up in poverty. Would you be willing to do some things with us to reach other children and get them out of the streets?"

In Matthew 11:20, it says that Jesus "began to *upbraid* the cities wherein most of his works were done, because they repented not". Let me see if I can help you understand what Jesus was talking about. Think of braiding hair from the back of the neck forward to the forehead. You know if you are a good braider you braid tight. Think of corn rows not from front to back, but from back to front. Ouch! That is what Jesus did to the church folks. The spirit of God says that we are at a critical juncture.

We are at a window of opportunity where the body of Christ is really about to be in a position to take over some stuff. We are literally in a place of revolutionary reversals. We are literally in a place where people who have not had a part in the mainstream, people who are on the streets are about to be placed in positions to make a positive impact on the whole of society. We cannot do that as renegades or rebels without a cause. You can talk about how spiritual you are, but you do not go to church. No. I understand what you are saying. You are saying that there are so many churches that are full of hypocrites, but when you find one that is not full of hypocrites, it is your obligation to unite with that church and work with that church to make a difference in this world. It is time for you to do that right now. I want you to be saved, to have an opportunity to not be a chicken, to not be a coward, but to have courage in God to be able to do the things we need to do to make things better for generations to come. That's wisdom.

CHAPTER THIRTEEN
IF HIP-HOP ISN'T THE ENEMY WHO IS?

If you want to get a hint as to the tenor, the tone, the direction, the trajectory, the purpose, the outlook, the perspective of this book, read Jesus' warning in Matthew 11:24: "But I say unto you that it shall be more tolerable for the land of Sodom in the day of judgment than for you." Jesus was not talking to the infidels or atheists. He was talking to the people who claimed to be righteous. He was talking to the self-proclaimed church folks of his day. We are living in some very troubled times. If there is anything we have no more time for it is playing church. There are things we can kind of pass the time doing, but we do not have anymore time to play church.

If you are not receiving in your life what you need through your church experience you need to do something different. As my grandmother might say, that is the God-honest truth. Anybody who stays at any church, for any length of time, and does not change for the better, or does not have an opportunity to change for the better, needs to do something different. Let me say that again: ***Anybody who stays at any church, for any length of time, and does not change for the better, or does not have an opportunity to change for the better, needs to do something different!*** That's why I wrote this book; to help you think differently.

If the church you attend takes an aggressive stance against the very people Jesus died to save, you should consider joining another church… with a quickness! If the church you attend teaches that hip-hop is our enemy, ask God if that's the place for you. Hip-hop is not our enemy. I hear you asking, though, if hip-hop is not our enemy, then who is? We have an enemy. It's just not hip-hop. It is not ThreeSixMafia. It is not gangsta rap. It is not Al Kapone. It is not Frayser Boy. It is not Crunchy Black. It is not D4L. It is not TI. It is not David Banner. It is not the pimp on the street. It is not the prostitute, but it is somebody.

You do have an enemy. While I am on this, the song says "it is hard out here for a pimp". Is that not the way it is supposed to be? What is the objection? Do you want the song to say, "it is easy out here for a pimp"? We are so silly. It is a good thing that it is hard for a pimp. That is why there are not that many. It is not the culture that is our enemy, but we do have an enemy.

The question is, "Who is the real enemy to God's plan?" not, "Who is the enemy to this church over here or that church over there?" A whole lot of *churches* are enemies to God's plan. Before we answer the question "Who is our enemy?" we must ask and answer another essential question first. The question is this: Why do we go to church in the first place? Is it to always be poured into? These are questions you are going to have to answer for yourself.

If I were to judge the way some people look while they're sitting in church, I would have to say not only do they not know why they're there, they do not even know who they are. So many people come to church on a regular basis, never engaging their emotions or intellect or bodies fully in the worship experience. Then they sit there looking at other people and criticizing everything and everybody there. They spend two hours formulating opinions for which on one will ever ask, articulating in their own minds what's wrong with the choir, what's wrong with the sermon, what's wrong with the person sitting on the pew next to them.

Does that describe your church experience? For you to come to church and still have a countenance of defeat is like a slow suicide. You're killing your own spirit. Or maybe you're a church hopper, you know, visiting churches all the time, and joining every one you visit. The reason you keep church hopping is this: You go to one church and you hear the Pastor say something you do not like, and you get mad. If you are a regular church-goer you need to start asking yourself, "Why do I come to church?" Is it to always be poured into? Is it to simply consume the blessings of God's word?

There are people who just love to hear preaching. They love it! They will leave church after morning worship and go to an afternoon service at another church. Then they will go home and watch T.D. Jakes, then Joyce Meyer, then Creflo Dollar, then Kenneth Copeland, then fall asleep at night watching Joel Osteen. We love the Word. Is that the only reason we come to church, to consume the blessings of the word? Do we come to church to receive a spiritual massage that soothes away our personal guilt?

The typical Black Baptist preacher worth his or her salt is an expert *message/massage* therapist. A Black Baptist preacher can do it, baby! He is so good with it he can put a tune with it. You've heard it: "*Aaannnd…* one Friday evening…they nailed his hands and feet…and buried him in a borrowed tomb…*aaannnduh* he laid there all night Friday night… *aaannnduh* all day Saturday…*aaannnduh* all night Saturday night, but I heard…" When you get to "I heard" – again, in the words of my Grandmother – "it's all over but the shoutin'!".

"Early Sunday morning…aaahhh!!!...He got up with all power!" (and then the height of redundancy:) "All power, in his hand". If you get up with all power isn't it a given that you have it in your hand? First of all if he got up you can assume he has all power. We – Black preachers – are experts. We can massage you until it does not even matter what sin you committed, but you shout and feel good. It is like a spiritual orgasm. That is what so many preachers are doing, engaging in ecclesiastical ejaculation.

So many of us preachers are not right; so many of us preachers are just acting. Then when it gets to the climax of the message everybody is just ecstatic and nobody has changed.

I refuse to oversee a meaningless spiritual orgy. If there is any ejaculating going on, somebody is going to walk away pregnant! Who's the enemy? Well, it could be the church, it could be the preacher, and it could be you. Here's one way you can get a revelation on it. Re-read this chapter. If it makes you angry, the enemy just might be you. It's not hip-*hop* we need to be concerned about, it's hip-o*crits* (hypocrites)!

CHAPTER FOURTEEN
A WORD ABOUT HOLY HIP-HOP

Since the advent of hip-hop, an interesting phenomenon has developed just beneath the surface of the gospel music world. Because the music of hip-hop, with its bass-driven melodies and rhythmic syncopation, is so infectious and full of energy, young people are naturally drawn to it. Hip-hop facilitates unfettered freedom of creative expression. The key word here is *creative*. The ability to create is rooted in our creation. God created us in God's own image, and by virtue of the fact that we are God's children we have inherited God's ability to create.

Creativity is the evidence of the presence of God in us. To be able to create something new and unique out of whole cloth is singularly God-like. To be able to do that with words, that *is* God. "In the beginning was the *word*, and the *word* was with God, and the *word* was God." Words are the stock-in-trade of hip-hop. When a rapper "spits" a rhyme he is doing the exact same thing God did when God first said, "let there be…" Not coincidentally, one of the most ubiquitous expressions

Hip Hop Is Not Our Enemy

in hip-hop is simply the utterance: **"Word?"** Words create something out of nothing.

Even when words are used to tear down or destroy they are actually *creating* an opposite reality from that which they have destroyed. That is why Gospel music's reaction to hip-hop holds so much promise. Gospel music's reaction to hip-hop is what is known as *Holy* Hip-Hop. The beats are the same. The styles are the same. The kinetic energy of the performers is the same. The look is the same. The feel is the same. What is different about genuine holy hip-hop is the lyrical content. The lyrics of holy hip-hop uplift, magnify, exalt, and glorify Christ. And whereas hip-hop motivates its listeners, in many cases, to pursue prurient lifestyles and ungodly activity, holy hip-hop motivates its listeners to pursue God's face.

One of the earliest proponents and moving forces behind the emergence of holy hip-hop as a musical genre within a genre is a young man whose given name is Delmar Lawrence. His stage name is "Mr. Del". He is now a licensed preacher of the Gospel, has his own record label, is signed to a major recording company, and is the front man for a musical group called "Holy South". He wasn't always such an accomplished person in the Christian world. Not even close. Delmar Lawrence was one of the founding members of the Academy-Award winning Memphis rap group known as, you guessed it, ThreeSixMafia!

Yes, Mr. Del helped write some of the most decadent lyrics imaginable about thug life in the streets of Memphis, hotbed of the "dirty south". He can tell you his personal story of transformation for himself, but suffice it to say that when he became converted to Christ he began to employ his talents to the task of spreading the Gospel in the form of hip-hop music.

Not long after Del established his group I invited him to come to our church to perform as part of a special youth event. He was being attacked on every side. The traditional church world attacked him for being a heretic, someone who was polluting the church with his "worldly" music. The so-called "secular" world of his hip-hop counterparts attacked him as being a "sellout". I didn't attack him at all. I wanted to encourage him to do whatever he thought he could do to help lead our young people into a positive existence.

The night Mr. Del & Holy South performed at our church was "electric". The sanctuary was packed with children of all ages, many of whom had never set foot in a church before. The parents in attendance had nervous looks on their faces, but as they saw their children fully participate in praise they loosened up. It was a party. The altar became a dance floor, and young people were all over the place "getting crunk"!

After his performance I called Mr. Del to the pulpit/stage (all furniture and podium had been removed from the pulpit) and laid hands on him and prayed for him. First, though, I taught a groundbreaking lesson on hip-hop. I based it in the scriptures and made it relevant to the hip-hop generation. Since you probably weren't there I'll try to share the essence of that message here with you because you're going to need to understand it if we're going to take back our streets.

You do know that if we're going to take back our streets we'll have to take them back from our own children, right? Trust me; they want to give the streets back to us! But they also want to believe we're going to make the streets safe for them. They want to believe that we will, in the words of the prophet Isaiah, "build the old waste places", "raise up the foundations of many generations", "repair the breach", and "restore paths to dwell in" (Isaiah 58:12 KJV). The teaching I did that night gave them a comfort level that they took from that sanctuary with them.

All good teaching begins with definitions. The following definitions are critical to a successful co-opting of hip-hop culture. Following each definition is a verse of scripture which makes the scripture relevant to the definition itself. Don't sleep on that word, relevant. If you think you're going to persuade our children to abide by Biblical mandates without making the mandates relevant to where they live and who they are, you are in for a rude awakening! Anyway, check this out:

Holy: set apart and identified as belonging to God.

1 Peter 1:16 - Because it is written, Be ye holy; for I am holy.

Hip: aware of and influenced by the latest fashions in clothes, music, or ideas.

Matthew 11:19 - The Son of man came eating and drinking, and they say, Behold a man gluttonous, and a winebibber, a friend of publicans and sinners. But wisdom is justified of her children.

Hop: to move quickly or lightly into, onto, out of, or off.

Isaiah 43:19 - Behold, I will do a new thing; now it shall spring forth; shall ye not know it? I will even make a way in the wilderness, and rivers in the desert.

Read over those definitions and verses again. Make sure you understand the connection between the definitions and spiritual principles contained in the verses I use to support them. Got it? Okay, now here's a verbatim transcript of the teaching itself:

HOLY HIP-HOP (or Hop-Hip Holy)

Young people, let's start with the hop. To hop is to do a quick leap. God is getting ready to allow you all to jump over a whole lot of years of man's vain tradition. You are going to leapfrog over some folk who have been in church all their lives. You are getting ready to walk into prosperity that folk who have been in church all their lives will not get. God is getting ready to do a *NEW* thing.

The new thing God is getting ready to do has nothing to do with the old thing. I have nothing against the old thing, but God says in Isaiah 42, "I'm going to do a new thing." He says it will *spring* forth. Is that not a hop? Church folk are taking their time trying to be careful, saying, "Well, we ain't never done it like that. Something might happen." Well, let it happen, baby. Let it happen. God says, "I'm going to do a new thing and it will leap forth." That is the hop.

What about the hip? See, I was thinking God wanted me to deal with it from the front (holy hip-hop), but just now God said deal with it in reverse. You know, flip it! Instead of holy hip-hop, teach it as Hop Hip Holy. "Hop" means you do not have time to be checking with tradition. "If mama and daddy don't understand it that is all right, but I gotta go. I know y'all want me to be in your church because we've been in this church all our lives, but there is no Holy Ghost up in here. I'm sorry. I love you, but I gotta go."

What is the hip? The word "hip" means fully aware of what is going on. Church folk can't play. You can't front anymore. These young folk are fully aware of what's going on and they'll call a spade a spade. If you are an adulterer, even if you have "Reverend" in front of your name, you cannot front on them anymore. They are hip. They know whassup. You cannot play church on them. They know the Lord. They know the Holy Ghost. You can act funny if you want, but they are going to *bounce with me, bounce with me* because they know what's going on.

Hip Hop Is Not Our Enemy

But what about the holy? This is where I'm going to lose some of my young folk. Thus saith the Lord, I will not require the sins of your fathers and mothers at your hands, but I'm holding you to a higher standard of accountability than I held your mother and your father because you have knowledge that your mother and father did not have. You cannot be a fornicator. You cannot be on drugs, hooked on alcohol. You have a higher standard. So bling-bling and hit it hard, but you better be walking holy. While you're bouncing, thus saith the Lord, "Do you think that just because God let your mama and daddy get away with that mess He will let you get away with it just because you have a do-rag on your head, a platinum chain with a cross on it around your neck, gold teeth in your mouth, a diamond-encrusted watch on your wrist, and a ring on every finger?"

If you believe God can save you from the streets then you believe God can save you to keep your body for Him. If He can't do it we're all wasting our time. Can I live holy? If I have the Holy Ghost I can. In the Married Couples class this morning many of us were sharing our testimonies about how our wives got pregnant before we got married and we got married just because of the good sex. Here's the bottom line (and ain't nobody gonna shout on this): Is God able to help me live a holy life? When you get through shouting, when you get through doing old school and new school and your way, the question is, "Is God able to help me say no to fornication?"

If I'm in the hip-hop generation and I commit fornication, is God going to be any more lenient on me than He was on my mama-n-em? I'm convinced that God has some things for you, our children, that we, your parents, can't get because we didn't do right. Listen to me parents, I don't care what you say. I don't care how close you are to God now. You didn't do right when you had a chance. We didn't do it right. But our children? God has some things for them if they stay on the road they're on now.

What God has done is He has accelerated their spiritual development to the place where they are ahead of many of us and many of us are twice as old as they are. Now you have an opportunity to prove that the word of God is true. Can God do it? Yes, He can do it because He paid the price. He died on Calvary. He shed His blood so that you could be in the holy hip-hop generation. (Attention reader: this is where the teaching ended that night.)

Before we leave this discussion of holy hip-hop, allow me to share with you a very personal moment. The following is the blessing I spoke over Mr. Del's life that night:

<u>The Blessing of Mr. Del (July 7, 2001)</u>

"This is an important night. Think about it: we didn't invite Mr. Del on a Friday night. We did not invite him on a night that is not part of the worship schedule of the church. We didn't have the young people as some kind of side show as though they are not a part of the church. This is our Sunday night worship service.   Listen, people say, "You couldn't understand what they were saying." Well, you couldn't understand "Ahhh…[traditional preacher chant]." You could not understand that either, you lying demon. You are just E&J. You are just envious and jealous because these young folk are free in the Spirit. I rebuke you in the name of Jesus.

I rebuke the spirit of man's vain tradition. I release a spirit of freedom in the Spirit that this world has never known before, in the name of Jesus. It IS so! Come on, Mr. Del. Come here, young man. Lift your hands, son. You are about to blow up. Thus saith the Lord, you are about to make some inroads even more so than you already have into a world that knows not Jesus, who knows not Pharaoh, who knows not Joseph.

You are about to enter into a realm where the Spirit of God is about to loose prosperity in your life, to loose some things in your life. He's got record companies. You don't have to worry about going to somebody else and asking them. He has birthed in you some CD's and some record labels and some deals. God says that He has already birthed it in you.

In the name of Jesus, I rebuke right now those demons that would try to hang onto your life. I rebuke those demons even now who are gathering around you, who are just hanging on just because they recognize your anointing. I rebuke those demons in the name of Jesus. Right now I affirm your spirit of discernment so that the Spirit of God would give you clarity on who to be with and who not to be with. I call upon your understanding in the Spirit that you will know that God is in charge and as long as you follow Him the devil in hell cannot rob you of your anointing in the name of Jesus. It IS so. It IS so." (The blessing of Mr. Del ends here.)

You know, that's not a bad blessing to speak over your children right now, if you have any. It's actually not a bad blessing to speak over yourself! If you're in the music business, especially, you need to re-write that blessing and put your name everywhere you see Mr. Del's name. Read it out loud and bless yourself. Go ahead; you have my permission to speak a new reality over your own life. You have my permission to become something more than what you are right now. You have my permission to embrace a new you. Go ahead, give birth to yourself! If death and life are in the power of the tongue (Proverbs 18:21) then you can kill the old you, and give birth to the new you RIGHT NOW! Do it!

CHAPTER FIFTEEN

CHURCH IS MORE THAN A SOCIAL GATHERING PLACE

Do we come to church with a higher purpose? From the pimp, to the player, to the hustler, to the thug, to the shorty that strips for a living, to the cat who slings drugs, to the person who grew up in church and wouldn't think of missing. Do you go to church with a higher purpose? According to the man of God, the prophet Terry Nance, author of the *God's Armorbearer* series of books, the church has a threefold mission: to transform lives, empower people, and release an army.

    1. <u>The mission of the church is to transform lives</u>. That is what the mission has to be. In other words there has got to be some change in the life of the person who is connected to a local church. How in the world can you still be at the same level spiritually that you were five years ago? You are in church every Sunday! It could be that we preachers are the ones who have been messing up. Maybe we're the problem. I am not

ruling that out, but if that is the case you have to look at the fruit. If all preachers are the problem why are there so many churches out here really having a positive impact on their communities?

The answer is that it's not the preacher's problem if you don't change. That part is up to you. And if the church you attend has not been conducive to your changing for the better, then why in the world are you still there? I hear you. "Listen Whalum, I know my church is not what it should be, but I've been in this church all my life. I was born and raised in this church. This is my mama's church, and my daddy's church, and my big mama's church, and my big daddy's church. All my brothers and sisters came out of this church. If I left this church my family would have a fit!"

Okay, reader, now you listen to me: "**Whatever, Man!**" Just remember that it's *not* your church, and it's *not* your family's church, and it's *not* your Pastor's church, and it's *not* the deacons' church, and it's *not* the elders' or the trustees' church either. It's *Jesus'* church!

How do I know it's Jesus' church? I *asked* Him. He told me to read Matthew 16:16-18. Jesus and his disciples were having a discussion about who he was and what he came to do. Simon Peter, who would later evangelize an entire nation of what would have been considered "especially wicked sinners", hit the nail on the head in answer to Jesus' question, "who do you say I am?" Peter said, "You are the Christ, the son of the living God", to which Jesus replied, "You're blessed, Peter, because flesh and blood didn't reveal my identity to you. You received revelation straight from God. And upon this revelation I will build my church; and the gates of hell shall not prevail against it."

The church doesn't belong to us; it belongs to Jesus. He built it, then He bought it with his own blood. Then He sent his Holy Spirit to empower His church to preach "deliverance to the captives, and recovering of sight to the blind, to set at liberty them that are bruised."

(Luke 4:18 KJV). If there is any group in the United States that has, historically, been systemically and systematically held captive; if there is any group that has been physically and psychologically bruised by the American tradition of slavery and its vicious institutional progeny, it is the group of people represented by hip-hop. It is the poor and Black offspring of the offspring of the offspring of the offspring of slaves.

These are the ones Jesus built his church to deliver and "set at liberty". And if there is any group in the United States (other than those who implemented slavery and maintain its vestiges today) that has, historically, been blind it has been the group of people represented by so many churches today. It is the mission of the church to transform the lives of all three of these groups.

2. <u>The mission of the church is to empower people</u>. Are we empowering people? Is your church truly empowering people? You have to answer that for yourself. To empower is to provide individuals and or groups with skills, information, authority and resources in order to carry out their responsibilities. Be honest; when you think of your church do you think of a place where you are equipped with the *skills, information, authority* and *resources* you need to carry out your responsibilities in this life? Come on, reader, it's just between you and me.

After the benediction, as you're walking to your car or cab, or down the subway steps, or to the bus stop, or catching your ride home, what life skills have you been given? What meaningful and practical information have you received? Do you feel confident in your authority to do what you need to do? Do you feel you have received the needed resources to be a change agent in your day-to-day world? I didn't ask you if you felt good when you left church. I didn't ask if you had a "good time today". I asked if you received the skills, information, authority and resources to carry out your responsibilities. I really need for you to answer that. Take your time; I'll wait!

Still don't know? Maybe the answer depends on what we understand the word *responsibility* to mean. Consider this definition: Responsibility is the social force that binds you to the courses of action demanded by that force. John D. Rockefeller, Jr. once said, "We must instill a sense of duty in our children. Every right implies a *responsibility*; every opportunity, an *obligation*; every possession, a *duty*." This is where the notion of "church" is so beautifully powerful.

Church is not just an organi*zation*; it's an organ*ism*, a living, breathing, active thing made up of many members. Think about it; the church is not called the building of Christ, it's called the body of Christ. And really, the church is not an "it" at all. The Bible calls the church the "bride of Christ", so the church is not an "it", it's a "her". And each church must operate fully under God's anointing in whatever realm she is placed. And each church has a responsibility to the realm within which she operates. A church that is made up of a particular race or ethnic group is responsible to meet the needs of that particular group while being a blessing to the community in which it is located.

I have heard many people say that "the most racially segregated hour in the United States is the Sunday worship hour", as if that is necessarily a bad thing. I could say a lot more on this, but here's my point: A Black church has a specific obligation, duty, and responsibility to the Black community that comprises her membership. That does not preclude that church from being a blessing to any and all other communities of people. The same is true for every ethnic group. So, I'll ask again: When you leave your church after the benediction are you empowered to lead, lift, and love your community in such a way that poverty and lack and ignorance and crime and oppression dissipate?

3. <u>The mission of the church is to release an army</u>. I don't know about you, but when I hear Jesus say that "the gates of hell shall not prevail" against the church that doesn't conjure up peaceful images. If

he meant what he said, the gates of hell do not exist in a passive, neutral state. The gates of hell are attempting to prevail against the church that Jesus built and bought. It sounds like war to me. And in case you think I'm just a loose cannon, somebody with no theological underpinning to my argument, allow me to direct you to another quote from Jesus.

In Matthew 10:34-38 Jesus says, *"Think not that I am come to send peace on earth: I came not to send peace, but a sword. For I am come to set a man at variance against his father, and daughter against her mother, and the daughter-in-law against her mother-in-law. And a man's foes shall be they of his own household. He that loveth father or mother more than me is not worthy of me: and he that loveth son or daughter more than me if not worthy of me. And he that taketh not his cross, and followeth after me is not worthy of me."*

This is not the language of a meek, timid, passive organization. This is the language of a commander-in-chief, addressed to his army. The mission of the church is to train and release an army. As a Pastor, it is not my job to try to make you feel comfortable in your mess. Some may say, "We ought to just leave it alone. We shouldn't antagonize the traditional church. It's not such a big deal that so many in the church condemn the hip-hop generations. Whalum, just leave it alone." What? Armies do not "leave it alone" when enemies have invaded their territory.

CHAPTER SIXTEEN
LET'S GO DEEPER

If it is correct to say that the mission of the church is threefold and that threefold mission is to transform lives, to empower people, and to release an army, then it can provide some guidance for us as we try to determine who the enemy really is. Whoever would prevent us from transforming lives, empowering people, or releasing an army is the enemy. It is not somebody that sings a song a certain way. It is not, necessarily, young Black men (and now, increasingly, young Black women) who wear their pants sagging down around their anuses. It is whoever is preventing us from transforming lives, empowering people, and releasing an army.

Determining who the enemy is requires constant vigilance, because at any point in time, the enemy could be us! The greatest impediment to an army being released is lazy soldiers. When I was growing up in the traditional Black church, we used to sing a song that really got everybody fired up. We would sing it to the cadence of a marching army.

The lyrics: "We are soldiers in the army. We have to fight although we have to die. We have to hold up the blood-stained banner. We have to hold it up until we die." If you are really a soldier you are never really worried about what the enemy does. Why? Because you are a soldier.

Fighting is what you signed up for. You know what a soldier does? A soldier fights. Some of you have given up the fight. Now you are trying to please your family members, co-workers, and friends. You try to make them think you are all right and you are still saved. To hell with them if they do not subscribe to the theories espoused by the word of God. Just because some people have been in church all their lives does not mean they are living their lives based on the word of God, but you do not know that if you do not know the word for yourself.

God has given the church today some detailed marching orders. We are part of an army that is on a specific recovery mission. We are ordered to take back what the enemy stole from us. We have been anointed to recover our communities and our children, not through pious platitudes and self-righteous indignation, but through fighting the good fight of faith. This mission cannot be accomplished with an army of scary, sensitive, stale soldiers.

The battle, hence the victory, is going to be a quick work, and if we are not ready for it we are going to lose. The battle lines are being drawn. Our enemy is not going to be the street. Our enemy is going to be the traditional church and traditional church folks.

Let me attempt to give you some clarity on my position with regard to the traditional church. I intentionally use the word "traditional" in my critique of the church. Church is certainly a good thing, and not all tradition is bad tradition, but when I use the word I'm referring to a specific form of tradition. I'm referring to *man's* tradition; more specifically, man's *vain* tradition, and I feel the same way Jesus feels

Hip Hop Is Not Our Enemy

about it. One day Jesus was having a little tête-à-tête with the church folks of his day: the scribes and Pharisees.

They were trippin' because Jesus' disciples had not washed their hands preceding a certain meal. Jesus retorted by pointing out various of their own hypocritical practices, ending with these words: "you have made the commandment of God of none effect by your tradition". That statement is found in the gospel of Matthew, chapter fifteen, verse six if you care to check it for yourself. That's really quite a charge Jesus levels against the church. What he is actually saying is that man's tradition is stronger than God. Read his words again: "you have made the commandment of God of none effect..." None effect? Yes, zero effect.

You and I can render the word of God powerless by our practice of vain religious traditions. What is tradition anyway? I'm glad you asked. The word *tradition* as Jesus used it has profound and nuanced meanings. And the word tradition as Jesus used it has to do with urban settings. Hip-hop is an urban phenomenon. It basically was birthed and nurtured in Big City, USA, in the ghettos of New York. Not coincidentally, Black churches have thrived in those same cities, even though they were born in quite a different setting: the rural South, in the throes of slavery and its effects.

If the Black Church is to thrive in the future it must do so in these same cities. If we lose our cities, we lose. Guess what the word tradition means, as Jesus used it. It means, literally, "the act of giving up, giving over, and surrendering of cities"! Additionally, tradition is that which is delivered from one generation to the next by way of oral transmission and actual precept and example set by a preceding generation. Man's vain tradition is based loosely on the written documentation of God's word, but is at once separate and apart from that written documentation in that actual religious practice supersedes religious theory.

Dr. Kenneth T. Whalum, Jr.

Or, put another way, action speaks louder than words. I can tell you from my own personal experience that most church folks, if given a choice between the way they've always done it and the way the Bible says it ought to be done, will always choose the way they've always done it! With regard to hip-hop culture I guarantee you that when you and I begin to really advocate for our children, and when we really get serious about rebuilding the walls of our communities, and when we really get excited about the economic empowerment of our people we are going to be ostracized and attacked, not by street folks, but by church folks.

CHAPTER SEVENTEEN

WHAT IS YOUR CHURCH'S VISION?

Okay reader, it's time to take a two-question pop quiz. Question number one: What is your church's vision? Question number two: What is vision anyway? Vision is a way of seeing. If your perception of hip-hop is that hip-hop culture is our enemy, your perception is a function of the way you see things, and if you are a member of a church your way of seeing things – your *personal* vision – is informed by the practices, precepts, and teachings of your church, or the church's *corporate* vision. Vision has so many meanings that I could probably spend the rest of this book unpacking them, but for our purposes let us limit our discussion to consideration of the following six possible definitions of this *pregnant* word, VISION.

Vision is the formation of a mental image of something that is not perceived as real and is not present to the senses. When you look at the young man on the cover of this book what do you see? What do you see when you look at countless other young Black men who look like him? Do you see someone who could be something positive that does not exist presently? Vision is a function of how you see yourself and your community. Every church ought to have a stated vision for itself as it relates to its community. What's your church's vision?

Vision is a mental image or impression given directly by God, which brings understanding of spiritual concepts. Has God revealed to you, through your Pastor, a mental image or impression of how things should be? Does that image or impression, as the church moves toward it, bring an understanding of the spiritual concepts you are being taught as a member of that local church? In other words, does your church have a vision which helps you to walk out the meaning of the theoretical concepts you hear preached every Sunday?

Vision is a compelling and inspiring image of a desired and possible future that a community seeks to achieve. In chapter one I shared with you this searing indictment brought against hip-hop by a Memphis Pastor: "ThreeSixMafia are pawns of the devil". According to published reports, this same Pastor called on his congregation to mount a "holy war" against hip-hop music. He also called on parents in his church to go home and destroy all their children's hip-hop music by breaking their CD's and erasing the music from their iPods. What kind of community vision does this kind of thinking bespeak? Does your community seek a future that includes positive input from the "hip-hop" generation?

Vision is an image seen in the imagination – a prophetic vision, a prophecy – an ideal plan, a conception of the future based on a wish or aspiration. Consider the prophetic trajectory imposed upon the church by the prophet in Isaiah 58:12 – *"And your ancient ruins shall be rebuilt; you shall raise up the foundations of many generations; you shall be called the repairer of the breach, the restorer of streets to dwell in. (RSV)"* The Good News Translation puts it this way: *"Your people will rebuild what has long been in ruins, building again on the old foundations. You will* *be known as the people who rebuilt the walls, who restored the ruined houses."*

Listen to The Message Bible: *"You'll use the old rubble of past lives to build anew, rebuild the foundations from out of your past. You'll be known as those who can fix anything, restore old ruins, rebuild and renovate, make the community livable again."* Finally, the King James Version renders the verse this way: *"And they that shall be of thee shall build the old waste places: thou shalt raise up the foundations of many generations; and thou shalt be called, The repairer of the breach, The restorer of paths to dwell in."*

Hip-hop is an urban phenomenon, a creation of the big city. These prophetic words from Isaiah definitely have an urban flavor and application. If the church will accept this prophetic mantle we can create a bright future for all our urban as well as *sub*urban and rural youth. Read those verses again with this thought in mind. I think you'll agree that the notion of "ancient ruins", "torn-down walls", "ruined houses", and "old foundations" are apt descriptions of most urban areas in the United States and around the world. But there is hope in this verse because it prophesies that the church has the power to "rebuild", and "restore", and "renovate" that which is in disrepair. This verse promises that we will "make the community livable again". I don't know about you, but that's good news to me!

Vision is a description of a desired world, always far greater than any individual or organization; described in the present tense, yet never achieved. The emphasis is on the aspirational or spiritual dimension of purpose, contrasted with goal, mission and role. Vision looks beyond what is and seeks to create what is not, always with a positive end in mind. It's always bigger than the individual or organization. The church's response to hip-hop must cease to be negative and condemnatory if we wish to emphasize an aspirational purpose.

Dr. Kenneth T. Whalum, Jr.

In other words, we should aspire to be more than we are and we are more than we have become! We should aspire to make our community more than it is. And we should aspire to help others to *be* more than they have *become*. Rather than condemn the hip-hop generation for who or what we think they have become, our task is to co-opt what is and create what is not. That's what vision is, and that's what vision does. And according to this particular definition, the aspirational aspect of vision takes precedence over goals, missions, and perceived roles.

Most traditional Black Baptist churches proudly identify themselves as "Missionary" Baptist. What if those same churches identified themselves as "Visionary" Baptist? How would that change affect the mission of the church. Vision informs mission. Mission without vision is merely busywork (activity meant to take up time, but not necessarily yield productive results).

The preceding definitions of vision are noteworthy and desirable, and we should strive to achieve as many components of those definitions as possible. But this sixth definition should serve as a caveat to all who would accept my challenge to become visionary in your approach to doing church. **Vision** is also defined as an apparition or fantasy. Failure by the church to take meaningful steps toward the empowerment of people to become better than they are robs her ecclesiastical pronouncements of their power and reduces them to little more than ghosts and illusions.

I have heard many times from many hip-hop artists that hip-hop, particularly hip-hop music, is merely "the **CNN** – Cable News Network – of the 'hood". They say that hip-hop doesn't *create* what's going on in the ghettos of urban America, it merely reports it. It's up to the church to help create some better news so there can be some better reports.

CHAPTER EIGHTEEN
WELL I'LL BE BAMM'D!

Our church, The New Olivet Baptist Church in Memphis, Tennessee, is a *Visionary Baptist Church*. Don't let the denominational moniker upset you or turn you off. If you have any negative feelings about Baptists left over from your childhood, trust me, the New Olivet is definitely not your grandmother's church. I won't take a lot of time explaining here, but suffice it to say that we are about as *untraditional* as a church can get. We went *through* the fire of church upheaval *to* the fire of Holy Ghost transformation to become a change agent in the South and beyond. If you'd like to know the whole story on that upheaval you can read my wife's book, <u>Destined To Be A Preacher's Wife</u>, by Sheila Whalum. Just Google it!

Our church's vision is to create wealth and leave wealth for our children's children. The seed text for the vision is found in Proverbs 13:22, *"A good man leaves an inheritance to his children's children."* The *community* ethos of our vision is drawn from the Isaiah passage you read in Chapter Sixteen. We consider ourselves "foundation raisers", "breach repairers", "wall rebuilders", and "path restorers". We feel called of God to make our communities livable again. The vehicle through which we pursue that calling is an initiative called Bust-A-Move-Monday®, also known as "BAMM!".

BAMM! is all about Black economic empowerment as a means of establishing wealth for the children of America, thereby strengthening the financial, moral, and ethical economy of America. BAMM! is our initiative to bolster Black-owned businesses as a means of empowering the least of God's people to determine their own economic destinies. On the first Monday in every month, hundreds of BAMM! supporters patronize a pre-selected black-owned business.

Imagine being a struggling or not-so-struggling business owner. Now, imagine literally hundreds of *brand new customers* walking into your business throughout the course of the day spending literally thousands of *brand new dollars* that you would not otherwise have received. Need I say more? If you'd like to know more about Bust-A-Move-Monday please visit the BAMM! website at www.bustamovemonday.com.

You may be asking a very pertinent question by now. You may be asking, "what does BAMM! have to do with the premise of this book, which is that hip-hop is not our enemy? What does Black economic empowerment have to do with co-opting hip-hop culture? I'm glad you asked. Come take a ride with me, will you? I want you to cruise through my neighborhood with me.

I grew up in an historic Memphis neighborhood called Orange Mound. According to *Wikipedia*, the website encyclopedia, "Orange Mound *is* an impoverished neighborhood in Memphis, Tennessee." I italicized and underlined the word *is* because Orange Mound was not always an "impoverished neighborhood". Again quoting *Wikipedia*, "Orange Mound was the first African-American neighborhood in the

United States to be built by African-Americans. In its early days, Orange Mound was billed as the largest concentration of Blacks in the United States except for Harlem in New York City.

The Orange Mound neighborhood (when's the last time you used *that* word?) provided a refuge for blacks moving to the city for the first time from rural areas. Although the streets of the early Orange Mound were unpaved, it was a vibrant community in which a mix of residences, *businesses* (emphasis mine), churches, and cultural centers flourished." Stay with me reader; I'm going somewhere with this.

One recent day as I was driving down Park Avenue, the main thoroughfare in Orange Mound, I noticed a once-thriving theater called the W. C. Handy Theater boarded up with plywood painted a bright orange. Then it dawned on me: the W. C. Handy Theater has been boarded up for at least twenty-five years! That means that my three grown sons, the oldest of whom is twenty-five, have never known that part of Park Avenue to be alive with commerce.

As I drove further, and noticed afresh the countless *other* former businesses that had been boarded up for the same period of time I realized, with deep contrition (a term which suggests that I accept my share of responsibility), that an entire generation of Black children had grown into adulthood thinking that this was how their neighborhood was supposed to look!

It is the same scene you see over and over again in hip-hop video after hip-hop video: Dilapidated neighborhoods… boarded up houses and businesses… broken down cars… filth in the streets… illicit transactions conducted in broad daylight… women and girls street-walking… men and boys (and now, increasingly, girls too) thuggin'. The young people who are making the hip-hop music that so many "church folks" object to, grew up thinking that their neighborhoods were supposed to have no life, no thriving businesses, and no Black community pride.

Dr. Kenneth T. Whalum, Jr.

At that moment I felt a prompting in *my* spirit from *God's* Spirit. Instantly, I knew that I had to do what I could to help revitalize my neighborhood, my community, my city, and my people through economic empowerment. It is only through economic empowerment that we will be able to rescue the next generation of Black youth. Economic empowerment is the unfinished agenda of the civil rights movement of the fifties and sixties. Economic empowerment is the *new* civil rights movement.

That day, driving past boarded-up business after boarded-up business, I received the idea for Bust-A-Move-Monday. One day per month we would raise, repair, rebuild, and restore our community, one business at a time, by patronizing as many businesses as we could, spending a small portion of the six to seven hundred billion dollars of disposable income of Black people in the United States. Imagine what would happen if every Black church would be intentional about supporting Black-owned businesses.

What reasonable objection could anyone have to strengthening the Black economy, which is a part of the larger, mainstream economy? Your church could do it starting the first Monday in next month! The size of the church doesn't matter. It doesn't even have to be a Black church! Yours could be a storefront church with ten members. And, by the way, have you noticed that many hip-hop music videos also include visual references to storefront churches? I'm thinking right now of Kanye West's ingenious treatment of "Jesus Walks".

The important thing is that Black folks and White folks would be working together, pooling their resources to do something positive that's entirely within the will of God. It's called *ethno-aggregation*, a concept I first heard from Dr. Claud Anderson (noted author of several books, including <u>PowerNomics</u>, and <u>Black Labor, White Wealth</u>) and it simply

Hip Hop Is Not Our Enemy

means the process of pooling resources to create, control, and maintain wealth, goods and services within a specific ethnic community.

Why Mondays? Because Monday is typically the slowest business day, especially in retail. Why just one day per month? Because *one* day beats *no* days! I'll be BAMM'd, and you can be BAMM'd too. God **BAMM** you!

CHAPTER NINETEEN

THE BLACK CHURCH: A SLEEPING GIANT!

It is the job of the church to build up the community by building up those who live in the community rather than tear them down through reckless and random finger-pointing and pointless pontifications. The real enemies of the church, the real enemies of our people are hypocrisy, poverty, ignorance, and such. Church leadership that does not attack our real enemies is not leadership at all. Let's not kid ourselves, though. An *awakened* church is not going to be an *appreciated* church. We are going to have to deal with some devilish opposition.

That's okay, because Jesus had to deal with some devilish opposition too. He certainly had to deal with a Roman government that did not take him seriously. They tried to disregard his authority. Pontius Pilate, the Roman official charged with disposition of the "Jesus" case, tried his best to wash his hands of the whole matter. But the most intense spiritual opposition Jesus had to deal with was from the established church folks of his day; the chief priests, scribes and Pharisees.

The chief priests, scribes and Pharisees were the keepers of religious tradition in the Jewish community. Jesus and his disciples (which means "learners who follow") made a conscious decision to separate themselves from vain tradition, that tradition which causes you to posture and act like you are living holy by going through the motions without doing the hard work of engaging in reshaping the community outside of the church.

Jesus didn't just *preach* to "especially wicked sinners", he hung out with them! He "kicked it" with them so tough that everybody was saying he was one *of* them! And he didn't deny it. That's our heritage as members of His church. We must embrace the "other" and love them with a transforming love. There is no doubt that God has placed an enormous mantle of power and responsibility on God's church.

There is no doubt that for this season, this time, this dispensation, God wants God's church to "rebuild, restore, and renovate", not through the traditional building fund to enhance its own physical structure, but through getting out into the community and making it livable again through systemic and systematic economic empowerment.

You and I both know that the Black church has the resources to make a difference out here in these streets. If you are still reading this book, you have a decision to make. You need to decide whether you're going to stay at a sleeping church; or whether you're going to help your church to wake up; or whether you're going to find a church that's already awake. If you're a Pastor you need to decide if you're going to take your ministry to the next dimension. Come on in; the water's fine!

But our task doesn't end with the church waking up. Once the church *wakes* up she has to *get* up, like Lazarus did that day Jesus called his name in the cemetery, and like Jesus did on the day he rose from the dead. What good does it do you to *wake* up, then not *get* up? If you're a Christian you believe that Jesus was crucified and buried. You believe also, though, that he got up from the dead. The question is what did he get up *for*? There can be no doubt that he died. It is an incontrovertible fact that he died.

We have to believe that he died because Easter is meaningless unless he died. He had to die so we could live. He died, and he rose. Is that not what the scripture says? Romans 8:34 says, *"Who is he that condemns? It is Christ that died, yea rather, that is risen again, who is even at the right hand of God, who also makes intercession for us."* He died for our sins and then He was buried. Why was He buried? He was buried because that is what you do with dead stuff, you bury it. If you don't bury it, it starts to stink.

A lot of us have a whole lot of dead stuff in our lives. We do not want to bury it. All that stuff from our past is starting to stink; stuff we used to do, stuff that happened in our family when we were growing up. We are carrying it around. It is dead. It should have been buried a long time ago because that is what you do with dead stuff. You bury it. It is all right to bury that stuff. If you hang around people who will not let you bury that stuff; if you have friends who will not let you bury dead stuff, even stuff in the church, you need to let those people go.

You forgot about it a long time ago. You put it down, but every time you go around these people they keep on resurrecting stuff you are trying to bury. Get your deliverance today and go ahead and bury it. It is all right to bury it. Once you bury the old you, you can get up brand new, and you can help create a new community, just like Jesus did. Jesus got up for our justification. That word "justification" means that God declares us not guilty.

Think of it this way: For me to be ***justified*** by Jesus' resurrection means that because Jesus lives, it is ***just-as-if-I'd*** never sinned. So we can get up, and move on, and do what we have to do on this earth and not worry about the sins of our past embarrassing us. When the church wakes up, meaning when church *folks* wake up, we can *get* up and *lift* up our community.

CHAPTER TWENTY

YOU'VE GOT TO PAY THE PIPER WHETHER YOU DANCE OR NOT

Several years ago there was a popular song by a group known as The Chairmen Of The Board. The song's title is "Pay To The Piper" and the chorus is, "If you dance to the music, don't you know you've got to pay to the piper. Ask yo' mama!" Well, I've got a word for you: You've got to pay the piper whether you dance or not! The hip-hop generation is crying out to us in a way born of their anguish. They created hip-hop to say what needed to be said about their world, the world we left them.

Jesus knew the hip-hop generation was coming. Listen to what he says about them: *"But whereunto shall I liken this generation? It is like unto children sitting in the markets, and calling unto their fellows, and saying, 'we have piped unto you, and you have not danced; we have mourned unto you, and you have not lamented'"*. At that time Jesus answered and said, "I thank you, O Father, Lord of heaven and earth, because you have hid these *things from the wise and prudent, and have revealed them unto babes." (Matthew 11:16-17, 25 KTW).* The last verse of the text says, "At that time Jesus answered and said, I thank you, Oh Father, Lord of heaven and earth, because you have hid these things from the wise and prudent and have revealed them unto babes."

If a baby can shout over the goodness of God, then God has revealed something to the babes. I am receiving e-mails from eleven-year-olds, twelve-year-olds, and thirteen-year-olds who are speaking things in the spirit that indicate that they have a deeper understanding of the workings of the spirit of God in this present age. They have a deeper understanding than a lot of the old preachers I have heard in my life.

Recently I ordered fast food from the drive-through lane of a burger restaurant. When I got to the cashier, a young lady no older than seventeen said, "Hey, you that preacher that comes on TV! I like you. I be understanding what you be saying." God is revealing some things unto babes. In many ways, hip-hoppers are babes, and I don't mean that in a pejorative sense. A babe is not just an infant or a child. A babe is a person who the world would say is foolish. A babe is a person who is not prudent by the world's standards.

A babe can be a person who does not subscribe to the theory of fornication, adultery, or stealing God's money. A babe can be a person that the devil laughs at. A babe could be a person who is going to do things God's way regardless of what their friends say. A babe is a person who refuses to allow man's vain tradition to block them from their destiny in God. A babe is a person who believes in God and wants to please God no matter who they might happen to *dis*please. A babe is a person who has made up in their mind that come hell or high water they are going to live holy.

On Wednesday April 12, 2006, as I was teaching **Keeping It Real Bible Study** (KIRBS) the "power that worketh in me" instructed me to ask the congregation the following rhetorical questions: "What good is my *Christian*ity if I cannot contextualize my *spiritual*ity to make a difference in my *real*ity? What good is my **Christian**ity if my ***spiritual***ity cannot change my ***real***ity?" (For that matter, what good is any spiritual discipline that does not result in the adherents to that particular discipline becoming better human beings?) In other words, if I cannot use my spirituality in the context of where I live every day, what good is it?

We do not live at church every day. I guess it would be nice if we could just live up in there every day, twenty four hours a day, seven days a week. For one thing somebody else would be paying our light bill. Somebody else would be feeding us, turning the lights on, locking the doors, watching our cars, but we cannot live up in there every day. What good is my Christianity if my spirituality cannot change my reality? My reality is where I live. I will tell you this. I have no interest in trying to serve a God who cannot show me how to change where I live every day.

Why would I serve God if I have to fornicate? If I have to fornicate what am I at church for? What good is Christianity if my spirituality cannot change my reality? That is a question I am going to ask until I die. How in the world can you continue in your mess and be up in the church on a regular basis? That makes no sense. You can buy tapes and do that. You can watch televangelists on television, and stay at home. You can watch television on Sunday morning if all church does is entertain you with a nice presentation from the word of God.

What good is church doing you if you can go right back home and go get back into bed with the person you're shacking with? What good is church if your life is not going to get any better? If I am a 'ho before church, and a 'ho after church, I can just remove church from the equation, put another 'ho there, and be like Santa Clause chanting,

"Ho, Ho, Ho!" because that is all I am! You and I have to keep in mind that we are responsible for the examples we set for our children and *other* "babes".

I am not saying all children are spiritual and have the Holy Ghost, but not all adults who claim to be Christians are spiritual either, nor or they guided by the Holy Ghost in their day-to-day life choices. While you are analyzing and criticizing hip-hoppers you may be missing what the Lord is trying to do in you. I want you to feel uncomfortable right now if you've been judgmental with regard to our children and the hip-hop generation. They are the generation "sitting in the markets" calling unto us, playing their music for us, trying to get us to listen, to dance, to understand, to act, just as the children in that Matthew text were doing.

Right in the middle of all that commotion, Jesus hauled off and told his Daddy, "Thank you." That is a special relationship if no matter what situation you are in you can stop and talk to God, your Daddy. You can be on your job tomorrow. If you're a teacher, and have a room full of unruly children, right off in the middle of it you can tell God, "Thank You, Daddy. I sure would not have chosen this. This sure is not what I signed up for." That is what Jesus did because Jesus was determined to allow His spirit nature to impact His reality.

Jesus was determined that His presence anywhere was going to result in a change. It did not matter where Jesus was. That is why He did not mind drinking with folk. While He was drinking, the church folks were talking. But the ones He was drinking with were saying, "You know, this dude is all right! I need to follow him and see what He's about!" It was not the alcohol. It was the Spirit that was already in him that regulated his behavior so that no matter what kind of wine he had in Him, he didn't overindulge to the point where the wine took control. It was his holiness that guided his life. It was not what he took in from the outside. It was not what he ate, or what he drank. It was what was in him all the time.

The same thing that was in Jesus as He walked this planet is in me and you, if we accept it, activate it, and let it operate. In John 7:38, Jesus says *"He that believeth on me, as the scripture has said, out of his belly shall flow rivers of living water"*. The next verse explains what he was talking about: *"But this spake he of the Spirit, which they that believe on Him should receive: for the Holy Ghost was not yet given; because that Jesus was not yet glorified."* The good news is that *now* Jesus *has* been glorified, through his resurrection, and *now* the Holy Ghost *has* been given and is available for all of us, and we can allow it to flow out of our bellies for others to drink!

What I am trying to get you to see is that you are supposed to be the kind of person who lives such a life that other folk get nourishment and sustenance from the way you live your life. In this way, you dance to the music of younger generations. In this way, you "pay the piper" because you're imparting to them a valuable asset: wisdom by example. Your church membership should be the means of your continued maturation in this process. The church is a spiritual manufacturing plant. Anything that is manufactured in a manufacturing plant is not intended to stay inside the plant, especially if they are perishable goods. (Need I remind you that your flesh is "perishing" every day?)

Perishable items will go bad sitting on the shelf. Your problem may be that you are not functioning in the way you were manufactured to function. The reason you get frustrated when you can't seem to acquire more stuff or make more money may be because you won't release or give any of the stuff or money to someone else. There is no room in you to receive anything more because you're holding too tightly to what you've been given by God. You were made to produce blessings, and in your producing you create a cavity and capacity to receive more.

Once you fill your car with gas, you do not fill it up anymore until you burn up what you put in it. God, deliver me from church folks who want to sit up at the gas station "topping off"! I spent a lot of time in Atlanta, Georgia and Philadelphia, Pennsylvania going to college at Morehouse and going law school at Temple before I came back to Memphis. At that time in those cities it was against the law to top off. When you fill your car up and set the pump where it is automatically flowing, once it fills up it kicks the pump off. It is against the law once the pump kicks off to squeeze in more. You just might need to quit topping off at church. Get away from the gas station and burn up what you have, then go back to get more.

The church is not a museum. A museum is where wax figures come in one way, stay that way while they are there, and do not leave [until they are removed]. When they do leave/[are removed] they are just like they were when they got there. As a Pastor in the twenty-first century I refuse to be a museum curator. My job is to put some heat, the heat of the Holy Ghost, to those wax figures. You know what happens when heat gets to a wax figure? It melts. It changes its form. If a wax figure stays in the heat too long not only does it change its form, it melts away. Stop tripping and do what you have to do. Whenever the devil is trying to get you off your focus do like Jesus did and stop and say to God, "Thank You, Daddy." If the devil is trying to get you *off* your focus it means that you are *on* your focus, so sharpen your focus.

So how do we sharpen our focus? Young people have been trying to get our attention, but when they express themselves creatively we tell them, "You are pawns of the devil." The young people are saying, "Hey, we are trying to get your attention! You need to dance!" They're saying, "We have mourned unto you. We tried to tell you, church, you have to do something to get our attention. You have got to embrace us, church!

You have got to let us in, church! And once you let us in you have to let us be ourselves."

Like the children sitting in the marketplace, our children continue: "But you did not lament." In other words you were so comfortable in your little thing that you would not be bothered with us. You let us grow up like weeds, church. Then you wonder why we put on ski masks, stole a car, and drove it to the suburbs. What the young people are saying is you have to pay the piper whether you dance or not. God empowers us through His word to do everything we need to do to get everything we need to get and to have everything we need to have.

Once we get it, it is on us to help somebody else to get it. God is holding us accountable and responsible, whether we want to be accountable or accept the responsibility or not. Have you ever had to pay a cover charge to get in a nightclub? You have to pay the cover charge whether you dance or not once you get in. Jesus said, "Whereunto shall I liken this generation?" I love Jesus because He is cross-generational. Just because He is a certain age does not mean that He cannot talk to folk who are older than He is or younger than He is.

You talk to people regardless of their age because, really, a "generation" is people who have a lot in common. It does not have anything to do with age in this case. Hip-hop is not our enemy, but it *will* be if we keep sleeping on the job. We owe it to the community to fix it so that the community is not such an awful place that those who live in the community have no hope. Stay focused on the babes. Keep dancing. Keep paying the piper.

CHAPTER TWENTY ONE

HAVE YOU HAD YOUR SPIRITUAL PROSTATE EXAM?

If your spirituality cannot change your reality you're wasting your time in church. Do you realize that our reality needs changing? If you don't, just grab your remote control any hour of the day and just turn on any channel. Look at our public schools. Look at our government. Come on now: You know I'm telling the truth! God really wants us to do a self-examination. Self-examination is not a comfortable procedure. Forgive the crassness of this analogy, but spiritual self-examination can be likened to what so many men loathe, a prostate exam!

When it is time for a man to get a prostate exam, there's really only one effective way to do it. They have come up with a lot of medical enhancements over the years, but seemingly this is the one area where there really is only way that they can, uh…still out of the many and myriad opportunities for medical science to progress into areas using laser technology and chemical diagnosis, somehow this area of prostate examination…still there is only one way. As much as I would wish and hope that there would be another way, there is only one way. If I am going to be checked I have to undergo the exam, and it's the most uncomfortable exam I can think of! God really wants us to do a self-check, you know.

I am just here to facilitate the self-check. I cannot check you myself, but as much as I can through the word of God, through the truth of the Holy Spirit I am trying to help you do your own self-examination. That is what He wants us to do. Really He wants us to determine again why we go to church at all. Are we really there to transform lives, empower people, and release an army? Consider the definition of the word release. It means *to unblock, to let something out that has been pent up or confined*. It also *means to make available to the public by distributing*. What ought to happen at church is that the Lord uses the Pastor to equip you and then make you available to the public.

As long as your Pastor is flowing in the anointing of the Holy Ghost, your exposure to your Pastor should result in you receiving what your Pastor has. You may not like it, but the world is looking to you to be who you say you are. The Pastor's job is to release you, to make you available to the public by distributing you. If the church is going to be what God wants it to be you have to start looking forward to being released. You have to say, "What does the devil have for me today? Bring that tail on. I am kicking that tail today." When you walk out of church on Sunday, and you are truly born again, and you receive whatever word God is pouring out in your church, you ought to have the courage to walk out and say, "Come on, devil! I'm ready to kick some devil butt! Shoot your best shot!"

If your Pastor is not equipping you with that kind of courage and that kind of skill you need to ask yourself what you are still doing there. If you still have to buy a video tape, or attend a conference, or read a book to get what you should be getting on a regular basis at your church, you need to ask yourself what you are still doing there. Let me ask you something: Have you made a difference in anything? Is anything or anybody better because of you? Are your schools better because of you, or are you part of the problem? When you get to class can anybody tell that you spend Sunday mornings in the presence of God? Are you making a difference in your classrooms? Are you trying to make a difference or are you trying to dumb down to the competition? Are you trying to be accepted by people you don't even like?

Remember the prostate exam. When the exam is being conducted the doctor usually says, "Relax." Then he sticks his finger up your…! Trust me; the doctor does not enjoy it anymore than you do. It's a thankless job, but it's necessary to keep the body functioning properly. In order for the body of Christ to function properly you and I must examine ourselves on a regular basis through submitting to the word of God. It is uncomfortable to be examined, but you have to relax and let the Lord do what He has to do. That is all I am saying.

CHAPTER TWENTY TWO

WHAT KIND OF ARMY ARE WE RELEASING?

What kind of army is the church releasing? Is the church even releasing an army? Consider the definition of the word *army*. It is a body of persons organized for war. An army is an organization of people organized for war. An army is also the complete military organization of a country for land warfare. What the church does (or doesn't do) affects the land around us. There are people who have never been to church, but they are essentially more holy and morally pure than folk who have been in church all their lives. These people are waiting on instructions. They're waiting for someone with integrity to issue some marching orders to recover our community.

Do you believe that we need an army? Do we have a cause? Is there not a cause? Like King David before me, I ask the question, "Is there not a cause?" Before he was even crowned king he was anointed to be king. While he was still a lad he volunteered to fight the giant Goliath. His own brothers laughed at him and accused him of grandstanding.

Hip Hop Is Not Our Enemy

To which David replied, "Well, I wonder why nobody else is trying to fight this fight. Is there not a cause?" We are having all this church in cities across our nation, and the streets are absolutely crazy.

We are building churches everywhere. We are in walking distance of some churches that look like the Taj Mahal …in the middle of the ghetto! Now they do not even tear buildings down. They add a bigger building to the big building! Is there not a cause? Does it bother you that our babies are dying in the streets at each other's hands? Is there not a cause greater than the cause of condemning hip-hop?

If the Bible is true then we are the salt of the earth. If the Bible is true we are the light of the world. How can we be salt and light when we stay in the salt shaker? If salt stays in the salt shaker then it is not affecting the meat around it. If the light switch stays in the off position it never illuminates the area around it. The challenge for the salt is to be shaken. We cannot get out there and have an effect on what is going on if we are not shaken out.

Even if you have a salt shaker you can hold it over the meat and turn it upside down and guess what! It is not coming out. It is going to coagulate at the openings. At most churches after the benediction all the salt coagulates at the opening. It is salt bumping up against other salt. We do not want to be shaken. We have to be shaken. That is all the Lord is doing to you.

If the Bible is true we make a difference in the atmosphere. You know what I think? There is really no doubt about this. I am not afraid that anybody can contradict me on this. You know the latest rash of juvenile crime, crimes being perpetrated by teenaged boys and girls? I think that most of us have some contact with those young people because we live everywhere. The people that go to church every week live everywhere, all over the community. Our children go to school everywhere. I am convinced that we come in contact with the children that are committing these crimes on a regular basis.

There is no doubt in my mind about it. If we are going to be an army, if we are going to accept our assignment, it means that we have to start living holy and being a light when we are at school, at work, and at play with other people. Our activity will affect their lives in a powerful and positive way. But it's not going to be easy. People who sign up for enlisted duty in an army are not expecting things to be easy.

In order to do God's will you have to cry sometimes. You want to do one thing and God keeps telling you, "No, I want you to do something else." You want to leave and God keeps saying, "No, I want you to stay." Or you want to stay and God keeps saying, "No, I want you to go." You stay up all night wrestling with God and crying and crying. Finally you make up in your mind "I'm going to do what God says do." I don't know about you, but I do not want to just spend my life in one place. I do not want to wake up ten years from now and still be at the same level that I am today.

I want to be better, but my definition of "better" might be a little different from most. Better doesn't necessarily mean having more stuff. My definition of better *includes* having more stuff for me, and God does not frown on me for that. In fact God promised, "I will give you the desires of your heart." Read your Bible; it's in there. God does not hold material possessions against us. He does hold our failure to help others come up to a level that He could be proud of against us, whether we have material possessions or not. In other words I can be broke, busted, disgusted, poor, and everything else and still be a failure in the sight of God. It is not because I am poor but because I am ineffective. It is not material wealth that makes a difference. It is wisdom in carrying out the will of God.

Hip Hop Is Not Our Enemy

If we mean it when we say to God, "Your will is what's best for me" then we have got to get to a place where we really are an army. We have got to get to a place where, as an army, we are ready to be released and move out and do those things God wants us to do to have an impact on the streets. Have you also noticed that the overwhelming majority of the victims as well as the perpetrators are young folk? Have you noticed that the suspects as well as the victims tend to be young people? In other words they are the faces of hip-hop culture.

You and I have to exercise wisdom as Jesus talks about it. We have to be wise in dealing with people who do not know God. We have to relate to people in a way that causes them to begin to make some decisions that lead to a better way of life for them. I don't know about you, but I am really happy about that opportunity. I am so excited about what is going to happen as a result of this book! The devil cannot defeat you. You're an army of one! You might have to go through hell and high water, but the devil is not going to win.

You are anointed of God to be a victor and not a victim. No devil in hell is going to be able to stop you from your destiny. We are an army! To the extent that we are an army we are in basic training right now. Basic training is the initial period of training for new military personnel. It involves intense physical activity as well as behavioral discipline. If we are just a group of folk getting together to shout and sing at church then we do not need intense physical activity or discipline. That is not who we are. We are an army.

Some folk signed up for all the benefits, but when they realize there are duties and responsibilities attached to the benefits they are ready to go AWOL (absent without leave). Everybody does not sign up for that, but basic training is for enlisted personnel. It is for everybody that signed up. If you are in an army you did not sign up for a bed of ease.

Dr. Kenneth T. Whalum, Jr.

You did not sign up to take it easy. You did not sign up to just lay in the bed all day. If you are in an army you signed up to fight. The only way we will get these streets back is to take them back. We have to make a difference. We have to fight.

(HAPTER TWENTY THREE

WALK IT OUT!

Not long ago my wife Sheila and I were having lunch at CK's Coffee Shop on Poplar Avenue, across the street from East High School in Memphis, where there is a community walking track. I looked across the street and saw a very interesting sight that was a spiritual revelation for me. I saw a father - a young Black man - with his two children. The father was not pleasingly plump; he was fat! He was fat, but at least he was on the walking track. His little girl was about four years old and she was fat too. She should not have been that big at four, but at least she was on the walking track.

He also had a toddler, a little boy, who was about two years old. They were out on the walking track together. This was in the physical realm, but I began to see them in my spirit. This was right after I started hearing this word from God about hip-hop culture and how it is our responsibility not to provoke our children to anger, how it is our responsibility to lead our children and to do for them, to facilitate them in the fulfillment of their destiny.

Here I see this fat daddy walking with his fat little girl and his fat little boy. All of a sudden, the little girl just took off running. She ran off and left her daddy. She was running so hard. She would look back and see her daddy and start laughing, then keep on running. Every now and then when she would look back and notice that she had left her father too far behind, and she would stop running and wait for her daddy to catch up. The little boy could not really walk too well. He would let go of his daddy's hand and take off trying to run like his sister.

Every now and then he would stumble and almost fall, but by the time he would have lost his balance completely and fallen flat on his face, his daddy had caught up with him before he could hit the ground. Daddy would carry him for a few more steps, comforting him, all the while keeping his eye on the little girl. When he got close enough to his little girl, she would take off running again, and the daddy would put his little boy down again, and they would continue the process. This went on for as long as Sheila and I were having lunch. What am I saying? It is our responsibility not to stop walking, but to supervise our children – the hip-hop generation – in such a way that they are encouraged to run as fast as they can and yet realize that daddy is never too far behind.

It is our responsibility to let even our toddler children, toddlers in the spirit, experiment with independence themselves. Let them listen to different kinds of music. Let them experience different kinds of things. They are going to fall sometimes, but just make sure you are there to catch them and continue the process. The mind-blowing thing of it all is that in the process of supervising his children, the daddy was exercising too! The end result of it all was that everybody would drop some unnecessary weight and get in shape for the situations that lie ahead.

Life is not so much about where you are as it is about where you are going. Do not get so comfortable where you are. Don't be the kind of person who worries God "to death" when things don't go your way. Don't continuously bug God to fix you up at a level that He does not intend for you to stay on. When you do that you're asking God to make you comfortable on a level that He did not design for you to stay at. He is not going to make it comfortable for you to settle for mediocrity when He created you for excellence. Walk out your calling, and help others to walk out theirs.

What makes this so important now, and this time in history? It's important precisely because it *is* now. If not now, when? When is God going to give us a next-step kind of instruction as to what we are going to do? That is what He is in the process of doing right now, through this book. Look at this passage of scripture again (Matthew 11:16-25). "We piped unto you…you have not danced. We mourned unto you…you have not lamented, but John came neither eating nor drinking and they say he has a devil." He came just like they thought he should have come. He had the church thing down. He did not drink. He did not trip, but they say he had a devil because he was weird.

Do you ever get talked about? Do they ever call you crazy? Jesus experienced the same thing. When Jesus came He came all the way from the other aspect with sinners. What did they say about Him? They said he was a glutton and a wino, and that he was no good. You cannot please folk. "Yet wisdom is justified and vindicated by what she does and by her children. Then he began to upbraid the cities." I want to talk about this thing where he says, "Then he began to upbraid the cities wherein most of his mighty works were done because they repented not."

Dr. Kenneth T. Whalum, Jr.

There is something very important that we have left undone in my city, Memphis. We have not repented. We are busy condemning everybody else and we have not repented for our own shortcomings as a city, and as a nation, and as a people; black folk and white folk. God is still holding us accountable for Martin Luther King, Jr.'s death right in my hometown of Memphis, Tennessee. We have not repented. We have not changed our minds. Black folk blame White folk. White folk blame Black folk. Then within the Black community Black folk blame each other.

Why can't we simply repent? All repenting means is to change your mind. I am not going to think about you like I used to think about you. I am not like that. I am not going to see you in that light anymore. I am not going the devil's way anymore. I repent because I signed up to be a soldier. When you are a soldier you are going to have to trust the people that are soldiers with you. You cannot be on the front line looking behind you over your shoulder all the time.

You have to trust your fellow soldiers, your comrades-in-arms. So put a hip-hop twist from Unk, a rapper from the Dirty South, on an old school concept popularized by my Uncle Wendell and countless other oppressed Black men and women in the United States who overcame their limitations with dignity: *"Walk together chillun, don't you get weary, and walk it out! West side walk it out, East side walk it out, South side walk it out, North side walk it out, now walk it out!"*

CHAPTER TWENTY FOUR
HIP-HOP THEOLOGY – HOW TO PREACH A KEEPING-IT-REAL SERMON

This chapter is a how-to chapter. I don't know about you but I get tired of preachers (and politicians!) who repeatedly tell us what we need to do but who don't show us how to do it. If you're interested in really reaching the hip-hop generation – and that's a very big "if" because I am convinced that traditional church folks and their Pastors (Remember, by traditional in this context I refer to man's vain traditions) actually have very little interest in reaching out and including the hip-hop generation in the life of the congregations – you have to demonstrate the principles you're trying to teach them.

Let's face it, most of us cut our eye teeth on television. We're a visual species. In other words, our brains don't really kick into gear unless we can match what we're hearing or thinking or reading with what we're *see*ing, both literally and figuratively. We've got to do a better job of using modern technology (e.g. playing music videos during sermons, or having deejays with turntables as part of praise and worship) and *techno-theology* to help our people *see* what it is God wants us to do with our lives.

I'm about to let you in on a trade secret, if you will. Preachers worth their salt all admit that they look at scripture through specific hermeneutical lenses. Hermeneutical is just a fancy word for interpretational. In other words, there really is no such thing as the absolute truth of the Word, so to speak. When you hear preachers say things like, "I believe it because it's in the Word!", or "God said it, I believe it, that settles it!", what they really mean is, "This is the way I interpret what the Word says."

Unless we were inside the heads of the ancient Biblical writers or walked the dusty roads of first-century Jerusalem (in the case of the New Testament writers) we can only do our best to approximate or guess what they meant by the words they used to convey their meanings. The process we use to do that is called hermeneutics. As a preacher who strives to keep it real, my hermeneutics are always tied to the relevant, day-to-day experiences of those I'm preaching to.

In the case of the following sermon, I actually played on our sanctuary video screen a music video by hip-hop mega-star Mary J. Blige. The video is for the song, "We Ride". [Go to your computer and get on www.youtube.com and search for that song. That's my jam!] If you pay attention to both the lyrics and the visual component of the music video you can pick up on certain hermeneutical principles that can be used to interpret any and all facets of hip-hop culture in a way that can enrich and add value to the lives of hip-hop adherents who are understandably wary of the traditional church.

Caveat: What you're about to read is a word-for-word transcription of an actual sermon series I preached, so read with your ears on, and try to experience the words as though you are sitting inside the sanctuary with us!

From The Day To The Night We Ride
Acts 8:26-39

8:26 And the angel of the Lord spoke unto Philip, saying, Arise, and go toward the south unto the way that goes down from Jerusalem unto Gaza, which is desert.

8:27 And he arose and went: and, behold, a man of Ethiopia, an eunuch of great authority under Candace queen of the Ethiopians, who had the charge of all her treasure, and had come to Jerusalem for to worship,

8:28 Was returning, and sitting in his chariot read Isaiah the prophet.

8:29 Then the Spirit said unto Philip, Go near, and join yourself to this chariot.

8:30 And Philip ran thither to him, and heard him read the prophet Isaiah, and said, Do you understand what you're reading?

8:31 And he said, How can I, except some man should guide me? And he desired Philip that he would come up and sit with him.

8:32 The place of the scripture which he read was this, He was led as a sheep to the slaughter; and like a lamb dumb before his shearer, so opened he not his mouth:

8:33 In his humiliation his judgment was taken away: and who shall declare his generation? for his life is taken from the earth.

8:34 And the eunuch answered Philip, and said, I ask you, of whom speaks the prophet this? of himself, or of some other man?

8:35 Then Philip opened his mouth, and began at the same scripture, and preached unto him Jesus.

8:36 And as they went on their way, they came unto a certain water: and the eunuch said, See, here is water; what hinders me to be baptized?

8:37 And Philip said, If you believe with all your heart, you may. And he answered and said, I believe that Jesus Christ is the Son of God.

8:38 And he commanded the chariot to stand still: and they went down both into the water, both Philip and the eunuch; and he baptized him.

8:39 And when they were come up out of the water, the Spirit of the Lord caught away Philip, that the eunuch saw him no more: and he went on his way rejoicing.

"We Ride" Series Installment #1

Everybody wants to find somebody they can ride with. I do not mean "ride with" in the sense of a romantic relationship. Why did I entitle this message, "From The Day To The Night We Ride"? First of all, because that is the title of Mary J. Blige's song, and I love that song. Secondly, because it is true that everybody wants to find somebody they can ride with. I am not talking about romantic relationships. I am talking about somebody we can share this planet with. Every relationship is not a romantic relationship.

Even if you are in a romantic relationship, chances are you spend most of your time with other folk in other relationships. If you are going to live in this world you are going to have to have relationship with other folk. It is a blessing to be able to find somebody we can hook up with. When I say "ride" I am talking about the rhythm of life, finding some folk that you have stuff in common with, being able to be in a community of people who believe the same things and who can grow, work, and make a difference in this world together. I am talking about rhythm, the pattern of living.

When I say all of us want somebody to ride with I mean that all of us together ought to be able to feed off one another and help one another. Membership in the body of Christ ought to allow us to make a difference in the real world that we live in every day. Come ride with me. Nobody wants to ride by themselves. I want you to ride with me or I want to be able to trust somebody enough to ride with them. It does not make sense to go through life lonely. Again, I am not talking about romance. Part of your problem is you are always looking for somebody you can hook up with, be married to, go to bed with. That is your problem now. What about just being able to sit up next to somebody that you know is not trying to stab you in your back? What about that kind of ride? What about the kind of ride where all of us can take an interest in children who may not have what we had growing up?

I am talking about rhythm. Your life ought to establish a pattern. You ought to fall into certain stuff in your life that gives you strength and energy. Some of you have found the secret, but you will not tell anybody else what it is because you are afraid they are going to steal it. Life ought to be a good thing. Find some rhythm. White folk have rhythm too. As a matter of fact, most white folk have rhythm because the rhythm I am talking about has nothing to do with dancing. The rhythm I am talking about has to do with prosperity and success in life and having something to leave your children and your children's children. That is the kind of rhythm I am talking about even if you cannot dance. I am talking about the kind of rhythm that will enable you not to die but to live. Do you want to live and not die?

Video Illustration: I like Mary J's song so I want us to watch the video. This is part of my liturgical presentation. Let me read the relevant lyrics to you:

> *From the day to the night we ride, we ride*
> *How you like it? How you like it?*
> *I see the future: you and I, better with time*
> *And it is what it is and I just can't help it*
> *And I felt what I felt and you know I just can't help it*
> *I see the future: me and you; that's how we do*
> *From the day to the night we ride, we ride, we ride*

Look at what it says in verse 26: **"And the angel of the Lord spoke unto Philip, saying, Arise, and go toward the south unto the way that goes down from Jerusalem unto Gaza, which is desert."** The angel of the Lord spoke until Philip and told him to arise. If you are going to ride with somebody you first have to get up. Some of you are down in the mouth, frowning, and sad about what is going on in life. Nobody wants to ride with a sad sack. You are around here talking about how you are saved, sanctified, filled with the Holy Ghost, and you never have anything to be happy about? I do not want to ride with you. You can *be* broke and not *look* broke. You have to get up.

The angel told Philip to rise and go toward the dirty-dirty (hip-hop terminology for The South). If you go to the dirty south you are going to

Hip Hop Is Not Our Enemy

get what you need. I am not studying these folk with regional bias. (The word *studying* is a southern colloquialism pronounced *studdin'* which means paying attention to.) When I was in school at Morehouse, a few people from New York and Chicago tried to look down on us because we were from The South. I said, "Your mama's from the south!" In many cases, of course, that was - quite literally - true!

(Video plays) This is for all the folk who think it is a doggone shame for me to use a secular video to minister: I am not trying to reach you. As a matter of fact, I am really not studying you at all. I am trying to reach these young people who watch music videos all day and all night long and who respect Mary J. Blige. If it takes Mary J. Blige to change their life, I'll use Mary J. Blige. It is about a rhythm, a feeling. If I can get these young people to feel about God the way Mary J. Blige feels about her man then I am doing my job. Did you hear what the woman said?

How you like it? How you like it?
Life is a mountain and I'm on the top

There is nothing ungodly about that. There is nothing ungodly about finding somebody you can share your life with and ride together, through the trouble, trials, heartache, and disappointments. It does not have to be a husband, wife, or lover. It can be a pastor, teacher, usher, or a choir member. The devil is a liar. You have to have confidence in yourself and confidence in your God. Did you hear the woman say, "How you like it? How you like it?" In other words she does not care whether you like it or not. Once you find God, the Holy Ghost, Jesus, it ought not matter what people think about you. If you know you are climbing the mountain of life then to hell with what the devil has to say. I am looking for somebody to ride with and I am looking for somebody to ride with me because guess what? When you say "Ride with me," that indicates you are going somewhere. Nobody needs you to sit up at the doggone stop sign with me. Let's ride. Nobody wants to stand still. If you do, find a church where they specialize in standing still. It feels good when you have somebody you can ride with. When you find out you cannot ride with them, it feels just as good to get out. It feels so good when you ride with somebody who is not going anywhere to say, "Look, let me out right here. Do not worry about how I'm going to get there. I can get a ride." That is what my wife Sheila used to tell me all the time when we were courting. We would be riding down the street and I would make her mad. She would say, "Stop. Pull over." I would say, "How are you going to get home?" She would say, "Oh, don't worry about it, I can get a ride!" That is when I would lock the doors and say, "You ain't leaving me!" It feels good to get somebody you can ride with, that you can share life with.

Again, I am not talking about romantic relationships. Some people who come to this church or who listen to our radio and television broadcasts do not really like my personality, but there is something about the atmosphere up in this house. People come here or listen to our broadcasts because they receive something that helps them go out of here and kick some devil butt, because we are riding together. That is what Philip did. The eunuch told him, 'Come ride with me, man.' The only people who are mad at you for riding are those who ain't got no damned ride! Damned in the biblical sense, of course!

Jesus paid for my ride. I can ride any kind of way I want to ride because I let Him get in with me one day. Some of you let the devil ride. An old song says, "Don't let the devil ride…" That is what's wrong now. You let the devil ride and now you cannot put him out. You try to unlock the door and he rushes to lock it back. You look up and he is in your lap and has the steering wheel. I am going somewhere and I want some folk riding with me that want to go somewhere. I am not trying to have folk ride with me that always have to stop every five minutes to use the bathroom or keep asking if we are there yet.

I will let you know when we get there. I am driving if you are in this church. I have a GPS that is giving me instructions, but I am driving. GPS-God's Personal Spirit. I just program, tell Him where I want to go. He gives me the short cuts, the detours, eating places along the way, rest stops, etc. You just ride like God tells you to ride. You will be all right. You have to be careful who you ride with and who rides with you.

This man was riding in a chariot. Nobody in modern-day society knows anything about riding in a chariot. I have another video (Reader: At this point I play on the video screen a CarMax commercial involving chariots). This is what Philip and the Ethiopian eunuch were riding in, but we are talking about our daily mode of transportation. When we talk about riding in life we are talking about your direction and how you are getting to your goals and your purposes in life. When we say, "Ride with me," it means "associate with me as I try to move forward in what God wants me to have."

You want people to ride with you who have something to offer you. You do not want to be riding folk around who can never buy gas or lunch. You all are spending more money on grown folk than you ought to be. A lot of you are hanging out with folk that you do not need to be hanging out with. You can be broke by yourself. Why would you be broke for two people? It does not make sense to me. If you are going to ride with somebody, ride with somebody who has something going on for themselves. Ride with somebody who is not a fake-phony-baloney-pseudo-semi-saint.

Ride with somebody who loves the Lord and who loves you. Ride with somebody who is not trying to change you all the doggone time. Ride with somebody who respects you for who you are. Ride with somebody who does not turn their back on you when things go bad for you. Ride with somebody who speaks words of encouragement into your life. Ride with somebody who has something good to say when other people are saying bad things about you. Ride with somebody who believes in you enough to pray for you. Ride with somebody who believes in you enough to try to help you make it to your goals.

Look at what it says in the verse: **"And the angel of the Lord spoke unto Philip, saying, Arise, and go toward the south unto the way that goes down from Jerusalem unto Gaza, which is desert."** Once you get down to the south you have to go down again. If you are going to make it in life, not only do you have to go down south, sometimes you are going to have to go through the desert. If you are going to Hollywood (a north Memphis neighborhood) from here and you are driving you are going to have to go through the desert. I'm sorry. There are going to be times in your life when there is nothing nowhere. You are going to be looking for miles around and there is not going to be a gas station, no water fountain, nothing to help you.

If you are going to make it where you are going you have to keep riding. Some of you feel like giving up, stopping, and turning around to go back the other way. I have news for you: it ain't time to turn around. It is time to put the pedal to the metal and let it roar. It is time to speed up, not slow down. If you feel bad now, if stuff is happening to you now, keep one hand on the wheel, throw up the other one and say, "God, help me make it through. I gotta make it." If you just hold on you are going to make it. You cannot be driving with your knee caps right now.

You have to keep one hand on the wheel and one hand in God's hand. God will take you where you need to go. Don't give up. If somebody around you is trying to make you give up, tell them to shut up or get out. You need folk around you that will speak life into you, folk that will make you feel better when you feel bad, folk that are going to lift you up when you feel down, folk that will point you in the right direction when you start to get off track. You need some folk that will help you hold on.

This Philip was not one of the chosen twelve disciples. You do not have to be one of the twelve to be somebody. I am so sick and tired of folk always talking about who they know, whose book they have, whose church they go to. Ain't nobody studying that. You do not have to be one of the twelve to make it in life. You do not have to have a special connection in order to make it in life. The only one you have to be connected to is the Holy Ghost.

If you have the Holy Ghost, the Holy Ghost will take you through whatever you have to go through. As a matter of fact, as long as you know Jesus, Jesus will put you in places where the folk cannot even put you. Jesus knows folk in places that nobody you know knows. If you will let God make a way for you, God will elevate you over a whole lot of other folk and put you in a position that you were not even qualified for. God will turn some stuff around for you, reverse some situations for you.

This Philip is first mentioned in the account of the dispute between the Hebrews and the Hellenistic disciples in Acts 6. There was an argument because the Hebrews, original Jews, and the Hellenistic Christians, who were converted from the Greek side of the ledger, started tripping, saying that the disciples were taking care of the Hebrew women and not the Greek women.

You have to watch folk in church. They will pick little-bitty stuff to get all upset about. They started accusing the disciples of favoritism. You have to watch folk. Watch their excuses and make sure that every benefit is available to everybody. Let folk cut them*selves* out of the benefit. Make sure the rules are clear then let everybody have a chance to follow the rules. If you follow the rules you can be included.

Philip was one of the disciples they picked to make sure they were being fair to everybody. That ought to tell you about Philip. Philip did not mind working. Give me a few folk that do not mind working. Take all the folk that always have a whole lot of yang-yang to say, but are not going to do anything. Lord, deliver me from a whole bunch of talking Christians that are going to talk and not do a doggone thing. Philip was a bad boy. Earlier in chapter eight, Philip preached so hard and was so cold-blooded that he was preaching and folk were getting delivered from demon possession. He was not afraid of anybody.

You cannot be a Christian and be scared. You cannot be afraid of these demons out here. You have to let these demons know you will open up a fresh can of Whip-A. As long as you have the Holy Ghost in you, you do not have to be afraid of a demon. Demons are afraid of you. Philip preached so until a sorcerer named Simon, who was a millionaire based on the money he was making from dealing with sorcery and witchcraft.

There are folk out here who will pay money for anything. Simon himself, the head witch, said 'Man, I want some of what you got. Bump all this sorcery. I want Jesus. I want to do what you do,' and got converted to Christianity along with the people who were paying him. Your life ought to be such that it does not matter who you hang with. Your boys and your girls ought to see the power that is on your life and they ought to want some of what you got.

Philip was so cold blooded that demons were jumping out of folk whenever he walked by. He was so cold blooded that demons went to bowing down to him when he walked by. If you have spiritual authority you do no care about any demon or what the majority says. You plus God is the majority. When you trust God, God will make a way out of no way. God will open doors when folk said you were not going to make it. God will give you a highway over your headache. Because of

Philip's history, even though he was not one of the original twelve, the verse says the angel spoke to him.

The big shots are talking about what kind of cars they have, who makes their suits, and where they get their custom shoes from. And while they were talking to each other, the angel was talking to Philip. While your friends are talking to each other, the angel talks to you. While your haters are hating on you, the angel is loving on you. While the enemy is trying to stop you, the angel is trying to block your enemies. If you just hold on to God and keep doing what God says to do, keep your ears open to God and after a while you will hear the angel telling you what to do.

The angel said to Philip, "**Arise, and go toward the south unto the way that goes down from Jerusalem unto Gaza, which is desert. And he arose and went...**" A lot of you would do a whole lot better in life if you would quit questioning what God tells you to do and just get on up and go where He tells you to go. The reason some of you have gone no further than you have gone is you are still *getting ready* to do what God told you to do. The problem is if God told you to do it, you are ready already. The more time you spend *getting* ready, you are blocking what it is God has for you.

And he arose and went: and, behold, a man of Ethiopia, an eunuch of great authority under Candace queen of the Ethiopians, who had the charge of all her treasure, and had come to Jerusalem for to worship,

Candace was queen of Ethiopia. She was a Black woman. That is not necessarily a good thing. You are not good just because you are Black. I know a lot of Black women that are not queens. I know a bunch of Black women that have no treasure and no authority either. Just because they were Black did not mean they were good. Just because they are White does not mean they are bad. It is not the skin color. It is what you do with the skin you are in that matters. If you just do right, it does not matter what color your skin is. I am glad for the purposes of illustration that this was an Ethiopian queen just because I happen to be pastoring a bunch of descendants of the queen of Ethiopia.

I want to tell you about this eunuch. Do you know what a eunuch is? It is a man who has been castrated, whose male capabilities have been somewhat reduced. A eunuch is a man whose testicles have been rendered useless. In the old days they would castrate a man, put his testicles in a jar filled with alcohol, and tell him to keep them because there was nothing else that could be done with them. When he died and was buried they would bury the jar with him because they believed that in the second life they would be back on, that in the rebirth they would be reattached. That is the man that was riding in the chariot. He was a eunuch.

The reason he was a eunuch is because in those days men who were trusted with the treasure had to be proven trustworthy. You could not have authority over the kingdom, have access to the queen and all the queen's women and be around trying to *hit it* all day long. If you are going to be a man of honor and integrity you cannot be trying to have sex with all the women you come in contact with. You would get further in life if you would honor and respect women rather than treat them as thought they were some kind of property. God would blow you up and increase you if you would just learn how respect, honor, cover, and protect women rather than try to have sex with every one you come in contact with.

There are a lot of husbands who are miserable right now because you try to maintain a dual lifestyle. You want to make love to a girlfriend on the side, but you want your wife to treat you like you are some kind of a king. You are disrespecting your wife. You are dating on your wife in the open, doing little stupid stuff. You know that she knows and you do not care. Well, God is not going to trust you with treasure, authority, and moving into the greater things of life if you cannot even respect and honor a woman. A dog is a dog is a dog. Once a dog, always a dog unless the Holy Ghost gets a hold of you or AIDS-whichever one comes first.

Don't be fool enough to believe all these women when they say, "You are the only one I'm ever with. I don't ever give it up to anyone but you. You are so powerful and mighty. I ain't never seen nobody like you. You're the only one I open my legs for." As soon as you leave the next man comes in the back door. You are the biggest fool I have ever seen in my life and every person she has had sex with, you have had sex with if you have had sex with her. You ought to be ashamed of yourself sitting up in the church, acting like you are proud of being a dog. I call forth a spirit of condemnation right now from the Holy Ghost. I hope you get a headache the next time you think with your lower head.

Men who are castrated at an early age begin to take on feminine characteristics. If you castrate a man before puberty, his voice never changes because you took away the testosterone producing element that makes your voice change and makes you develop male characteristics. This Ethiopian eunuch had authority over the treasury, he was riding, reading the Bible. You can say what you want to, but he was over all the money-while you are tripping and thinking he must be gay.

That is your problem. He is over all the money, he is a man of great authority (usually they were castrated because they did not want to be people who could not be trusted, because they wanted to give their lives in service to God and did not want to be distracted by their flesh), yet you are calling him gay when he is the one being trusted with all of the treasure of the queen of Ethiopia. You are sitting up with two dimes in your pocket, trying to act like you have something and are going somewhere. If you get home it is going to be in some woman's car. If you eat it is going to be because some woman buys your lunch. You do not have anything and are not going anywhere, but you are tripping about the Ethiopian eunuch. Man, please.

This man had been castrated. He had feminine characteristics. When you castrate a man at an early age, the long bone growth does not stop. In other words your legs get longer than a normal person's so he is taller than everybody else. When he is castrated at an early age he does not have broad shoulders. He cannot develop muscle properly. He is weak-looking. He does not have hair on his skin, smooth-skinned like a woman, looking all effeminate, yet he is in charge of the treasury. You are tripping because he has a high voice and these feminine characteristics yet he has sense enough, even with the things that have gone on in his life, to be reading the word of God. You do not even know where your Bible is. This man at least knew enough to read the word of God to get him where he wanted to go in life. He knew the word of God so well that at least he recognized when a man of God had walked up to his carriage. Some of you do not even recognize a man of God when he is in your pulpit.

The first person you should not let ride with you is the low rider. Do you remember that song? Proverbs 29:23 "A man's pride shall bring him low, but honor shall uphold the humble in spirit." Do not let people who are too prideful take too prominent a place in your life. People who are filled with ungodly pride will end up being low. When a prideful person is low they are not just low, they are low-down. While you are trying to maintain a spirit of humility, if you associate yourself with overly prideful people, they will begin to try to make you feel less than you are because of the fact that God has taken them down a few notches. Do not let the low rider ride with you.

"We Ride" Series Installment #2

Some might wonder why I do series all the time. The word of God is so loaded that you really cannot do justice to any passage with one treatment, particularly in a limited time frame. I really do not care what people think of me as long as the word is being put out straight, uncut, no chaser and as long as lives are being changed. I am trying to figure out now how I can do a series that lasts fifty-two Sundays. It just has not come to me. The Lord has not allowed me to do it, but if the Lord says the same I am going to do whatever I need to do to help men and women, boys and girls change their minds and do right because everybody needs to make up their mind to do right.

Recap: Everybody wants to find somebody they can ride with in life, somebody they can share this planet with. This is not referring to romantic relationships. If I was just talking about romantic relationships some of us would never be happy. The truth of the matter is that some of us are not meant to ride with anybody romantically. God is waiting for some of us to demonstrate loyalty and faithfulness to God before He will trust us with somebody else to be loyal and faithful to.

We are not necessarily talking about romantic relationships. We are talking about hooking up with people of like minds to accomplish positive things together. When you say, "I'm looking for somebody to ride with," you are talking about hooking up with a group of folk who are sharing with you in your desire to do something good in life. you do not need to ride with folk who are going to pull you down.

It is about establishing a rhythm in life. Rhythm is defined as a regularly occurring pattern of activity, for example, cycle of the seasons. In life you want to hook up with folk and ride with folk who can be with you through the ups and the downs. In life you ought to be searching for people who you can share this planet with, who can help you when you need help and who you can help when they need help. When you talk about riding with somebody you talk somebody you can share life's vicissitudes with you, the cycles and seasons of life.

Things happen in life, good and bad and you need a group of folk you can share the cycles of life with. Do you have anybody in your life that you do not have to worry about them begging for stuff all the doggone time? Thank God that you have somebody to ride with.

Not only does rhythm indicate a pattern of regularly occurring activity. It also indicates a pattern suggesting movement. You do not need to establish a rhythm with somebody that is not going somewhere. You do not need to establish close relationship with folk that do not want anything, do not have anything, are not going anywhere, and are nobody. You want to hook up with some folk that are doing better than you are, that are riding a little bit better than you are, that can inspire you to do better in life.

You do not need to ride with anybody that is taking you back where you have been. You need to ride with somebody who is going to drop you off somewhere you need to go. You have to be careful who you let ride with you. Some of you have taken on some folk, gave them your last name, and now you are stuck riding with somebody who has the same last name, but you are going in two different directions.

There are some folk you do not need to let ride with you and there are some folk you do not need to ride with. The first one you do not need to let ride with you is the low rider. We see in the scripture that pride will bring you low (Proverbs 29:23). You do not need to hook up with folk who are so prideful they cannot see the forest for the trees. Folk who are filled with too much pride think they are high when they are really low.

[Illustration: Mary J. Blige video shows Mary riding her motorcycle in one lane, and her boyfriend riding his in another.] …In life you have to stay in your lane. This is hip hop theology. The only time you need

Hip Hop Is Not Our Enemy

to change lanes in life is when you need to make a turn up ahead or when you need to pass somebody who is slowing you down. In other words you are in a course of action in your life where you are stuck in traffic and you have surpassed folk who you used to be behind in your spiritual walk. You do not need to be stuck behind somebody who is behind you in the spirit. Some of you do not want to pass folk because you do not want to hurt their feelings.

Your problem is you changed lanes, you accelerated, and got ready to pass, but then somebody caught your eye and made you feel ashamed because they know you are getting ready to pass them. So they started talking about you, saying things like, "You are better than everybody now. Oh, mama's church ain't good enough for you anymore…yang, yang, yang and yackedy, yackedy, yack." So you slowed back down to get back behind somebody that is going nowhere!

You have to be on the lookout for folk who are going the same way you are going and who are riding just as cool as you are riding. You have to realize that just because God has blessed you does not mean He is not blessing somebody else. Do not ever think that because God has blessed you with a certain level of physical things, material wealth, that somebody else is not doing better than you are. As a matter of fact, you ought to be seeking and searching out folk that are doing better than you are so they can help you do better than you are doing.

Always realize that God is so big, His ways are not our ways, and while He is blessing you over here He is steady blessing somebody else. Once you identify somebody who is going in the direction you are going, you establish a rhythm together. See, you do not hook up too soon. I am not talking about romantic relationships although it does fit. You ride a while. You see how they react to problems, yield signs, stop signs, red lights, and inclement weather. Anybody can ride cool when it is sunny and seventy-two degrees. The test comes in when it

Dr. Kenneth T. Whalum, Jr.

is raining and dark. Do you still ride as carefully as you did when the sun was shining? You all have some decisions to make about who you are riding with…

She said, "I have a song in my heart." Baby, listen: if you are going to make it in life, you better find a song and have one in your heart. If your memory is bad and you cannot remember the song, you better make one up on the spot. When the going gets tough you better make one up. Mary J. said, "I'll sing it a capella. I'll sing it to the beat." "A capella" means there are going to be times in your life when you have no accompaniment, when there is no drummer keeping the beat, no bass player holding that bottom down, no rhythm guitar giving it some soul. You are not going to have anything else, but you are still going to have to sing a song God gave you in your heart. You have to sing it a capella. She said, "I'll sing it to the beat." In other words God is going to bless you. You are not always going to have to sing it by yourself. God is going to send you some folk who will hold that bottom, keep the rhythm, and allow you to improvise.

I love jazz music so much because jazz is an indigenous art form that was created by Black folk in America and the lynch pin to jazz is improvisation. As long as somebody is keeping the beat you are free to solo however you feel. Baby, that is the stage I am at in my life right now. I am just soloing. I do like I feel, play what I want to. God will bless you to ride with folk who will support you in the achievement of your destiny.

God is going to bless you so you can ride in association with folk. You can ride through the tunnels of life with some folk. There are sometimes when it is really dark around you, but if you keep your head up and keep looking ahead you will always be able to identify the light at the end of the tunnel.

When you find somebody to ride with who is supportive of you [would you not spend every dime, every cent on that person]? Here is what the playa-playa from the Himalayas are saying right now: "Hey, dog. Look here-I ain't spendin' every dollar, every cent on no gal, on no woman, you know-ah-mean? She gonna have to take care of me." Baby, if you are with that kind of Negro [get away from him]. Let me help the young boys: when you find a woman that turns you on, that is everything you thought you wanted, boy, you do not mind spending money. You ask, "How much do you need?"

If you have found a church that nurtures you, you ought not have a problem paying your tithes, offerings, everything above the tithes and offerings because the church is meeting your needs. If what I do is of value to you, the Bible says the laborer is worthy of his hire. Nobody minds except old stingy, small-minded men anyway. Women do not typically have a problem with the pastor living well, dressing well, and looking good. They like that. When you are riding with somebody who supports you, you have no problem spending your money, using your resources to support it.

They touched hands while they were riding. They bumped fists. Every now and then if you have found a group of folk you can ride with, you do not mind showing signs that you appreciate the people you ride with. I have been a part of a church where folk just talked about each other all the doggone time, where you had a clique over here, talking about the clique over here, which was talking about the clique over here. Then you had a situation where she was dating this woman's husband, he was dating this man's wife, and that was accepted behavior. We are in a situation where holiness is the standard. I did not say there is not some mess going on. I said mess is not the accepted standard in this house. It is holiness or hell. I am not going to lead with an example of mess.

Dr. Kenneth T. Whalum, Jr.

The rhythm I am talking about with a church or people who support you is so cold-blooded because when you are flowing in a way that God wants you to flow in your life, you are helping other people, and other people are helping you, stuff starts happening that does not even fit together. What in the world is Mary J. Blige, the queen of hip hop doing fronting a thirty-piece orchestra, with cellos, violins, and a conductor. That does not even go together, but God will fix it so that in spite of your upbringing, background, God will elevate you and lift you into another dispensation where these things happen.

Mary says, "I see the future in you; that's how we do. I see the future; we're better with time." You have to find somebody to ride with, with whom you can get [that benefit]. Can you realize there are some areas where you need to do better?

I need to say a word about Candace, Philip, and the eunuch. We did a background check on Philip. We found out that the eunuch asked Philip to ride with him in spite of the fact that Philip was a renegade. Philip was on the run for doing things right. When you do things right folk are not going to just let you be. You wonder why you are catching hell on your job all of a sudden. It is not all of a sudden. Your enemies on your job have been watching you. They have been noticing that some of the mess you used to get involved, you do not mess with anymore and the devil decided he was going to make an example out of you.

There are some of us who are going through horrendous stuff. Tiffany was in a significant, terrible car crash the other day. If you look at the car it is a wonder that she is alive, but she *is* alive and has no broken bones or anything. Just last night Derwayne Trahan were at Burger King at 9:30 when a group of folk broke in and robbed the Burger King. They had them all on the floor. Derwayne said nothing happened to them. They just started praying to them out loud while they were on the floor. This is not just happenstance. These are no accidents. These are attacks of the enemy, but they are opportunities God is giving you to be who you say you are. Something is getting ready to happen in your life that is not going to hurt you, but help you identify who you are. In other words you are not going to be able to ride incognito anymore. You are busted. There is nothing like being somewhere you think nobody knows you then somebody walks up and says, "Ain'tchu a Olive?"

8:26 And the angel of the Lord spoke unto Philip, saying, Arise, and go toward the south unto the way that goes down from Jerusalem unto Gaza, which is desert.

8:27And he arose and went: and, behold, a man of Ethiopia, an eunuch-A eunuch is a man who has been castrated, no longer has the use of his testes. He no longer can engage in sexual activity. The word eunuch means "bed keeper" literally. In those days men who were eunuchs were trusted with great authority because everybody knew they could not be up on the women. They were not interested in women. Another thing we said about the eunuch was because of his castration at an early age he had probably developed many feminine characteristics. Not only that, but he was taller than most men because when you are castrated at an early age you do not have the testosterone that would have checked the growth of your legs. Your legs get much longer than those of an ordinary man.

This man was not only tall and effeminate, he had no muscle. He also had no hair on his skin. According to science eunuchs are moody. As a matter of fact they have a temperament a lot like a woman's. There is no testosterone. There is nothing to check all of that. So here he is, an effeminate man with a high voice, reading the Bible out loud. Imagine how we would have sounded reading aloud. Our culture has some of us laughing at that person, but if a person has been castrated, that person had no choice over that.

A lot of people you laugh at did not have any choice in how they got the way they are. A lot of times the person who would laugh at that person would also be the kind of person who would abuse that person at an early age. There is something about the psyche (there is a lot of study to back this up) that causes that child to actually act out the thing that he hates the most. We cannot understand why that is. We know that the devil is involved whenever there is any kind of sexual abuse, especially of a child. We cannot hold that child culpable and responsible for something that happened to him or her over which he/she has absolutely no control.

What we have to do is be like Philip. Instead of judging people based on our culture and based on what people say and think, we have to be willing to obey the voice of the Lord. The angel of God told Philip, "Get up and go join yourself to this chariot." The typical man would say, "I ain't riding with no punk." You are making a whole lot of assumptions and do not know what the hell you are talking about. If there is any place that ought to help us understand how things work in real life it ought to be the church, but so many times the church is the one perpetuating the ignorance we perpetuate against our own people.

Candace is the queen of Ethiopia, an African country. Ethiopia was well known for wealth. It was a center of commerce. I just say that because it feels so good to know that Candace looked like my wife Sheila. It feels so good to know that Candace looked like these babies up here. It feels so good to know that in spite of what happened in the Ethiopian eunuch's past, he was entrusted with the treasure of the queen of Ethiopia. Say what you want to, that is power right there. You have to stop listening to what folks say and start watching how they are living.

Hip Hop Is Not Our Enemy

Stop letting other folk's opinions determine what you believe about another person. You have to begin to ride with folk who have no airs are not putting on fronts, who believe in being honest and just, and living lives of integrity. You ought to ride with somebody and let them be who they are as long as they are going to let you be who you are. As long as you do not try to change me I am not going to try to change you. Let's ride.

The second person you do not need to let ride with you is the dirty rider. Some of you would be all right if you would quit letting these dirty riders ride with you. Psalm 24:3-6: 3Who shall ascend into the hill of the LORD? or who shall stand in his holy place?

4He that hath clean hands, and a pure heart; who hath not lifted up his soul unto vanity, nor sworn deceitfully.

5He shall receive the blessing from the LORD, and righteousness from the God of his salvation.

6This is the generation of them that seek him, that seek thy face, O Jacob. Selah

A dirty rider is a person who always has their hands in somebody else's business. A dirty rider is somebody who every time you talk to them they have somebody else's name, situation, and relationship on their mouth. A dirty rider is not necessarily a person who has engaged in criminal activity, but a person whose mouth indicates that their heart is not right. You have to stop letting folk ride with you who are always making disparaging remarks about other people, even in the church.

The church is notorious for folk who put their mouths on other folk in business they know nothing about. You are around here repeating what you heard some other dirty rider say. If you are not in the situation and do not know what is going on, keep your silly mouth shut. You do not have to repeat stuff just because somebody told you. You let them fool you by saying they know a close friend of a close friend of a close friend of the person they are talking about. You idiot. They do not know what the hell they are talking about. You need to close your ears when they start talking that yang-yang. Nobody wants to hear all that garbage.

You can always find something untoward to speak about somebody else. You will always hear some stuff that is not right. That does not mean you have to have your nose up in somebody else's business and you certainly ought to keep your opinion to your doggone self. How dare you put your mouth on somebody that you are not sleeping with at night? How dare you be spreading malicious gossip about people that you do not even know? You better quit letting these dirty riders ride with you because when you let a dirty rider ride with you, you are dirty too.

The song "Dirty Rider" is talking about how the police are trying to catch him with illegal drugs, weapons, and/or contraband. Did you know that if you have somebody riding with you and the police stop you (for any reason) and if your passenger is possessing anything illegal, guess who is going to jail. You are going to jail. You have to be careful who you ride with and who you let ride with you. God is going to hold you responsible for the associations you maintain.

I ran into a young man recently who said to another young man that he cannot find a woman in the clubs and these women are so shallow. The other young man knew who I was and you could tell he was trying to check him. Dude kept on talking. The other young man said, "How are you going to find a wholesome woman at a club? If you want to have a chance that the woman has something going on, you have to go to church." It is all about trying to find some folk you can ride with that can help you get where you are going. That is all I am saying.

"We Ride" Series Installment #3

Everybody wants to find somebody they can ride with in life. It is a shame that so many of us are lonely. I am not talking about "lonely" in the sense of not having a man or a woman. Trust me, saints, there are some married folk that are lonely. It has something to do with an inner journey. I have some single folk in [my congregation] who live by themselves and are not lonely. There is no need in us having attitudes with each other because we are desirous of their state of affairs. It is about hooking up with somebody in your life that you can share things in common with, other people who believe what you believe and are not going to hurt you. That is a wonderful thing. That is the premise of this whole series of messages.

Everybody wants to find somebody they can ride with in life, somebody they can share this planet with. This is not referring to romantic relationships. To ride means to be hooked up with people of like minds and to accomplish positive things together. It is about establishing a rhythm in life. A rhythm is a regularly occurring pattern of activity. You have to get plugged into something. Those of you who come to church every now and then (you hit it and quit it) or you come on Sunday mornings but do not come on Sunday nights, are breaking the rhythm. By breaking the rhythm you are holding a lot of us back.

[Live Illustration: walking in rhythm with two people in the sanctuary; one broke rhythm] He broke the rhythm...[walking in rhythm with two other people who stayed in rhythm]. There is nothing like folk going the same direction at the same pace with nobody stopping, doing what they want to do. It is about establishing a rhythm. When you choose to break away from the group you are interfering with the rhythm...We are moving in slow motion. Every time we get a group of folk together with a good idea and a good future somebody in the group decides [to break the rhythm].

Dr. Kenneth T. Whalum, Jr.

> ***MARY J. BLIGE*** *"We Ride (I See The Future)"*
> *From the day To the night We ride We ride We ride*
> *Hey How you Like it How you Like it*
> *I see The future baby You and I Better with time*
> *And it is What it is And I Just can't help it*
> *I see the future, baby Me and you That's how we do.*

Mary J. was doing fine by herself. You do not just have to be hooked up with any individual. Mary had her own motorcycle helmet with her initials on it, matching outfit, matching motorcycle-she is doing fine. I can do bad all by myself, but I can also do good all by myself. If being with me is going to cause me to do bad I choose to do good by myself. That goes for all types of relationships. You do not have to be with anybody. If you do not have a rhythm you do not achieve your purpose. Our church is unique, which means one of a kind. Here at this church we have a plan and it is called, "Sunday Morning, Sunday Night, Wednesday Night." What is the Plan? A plan is a proposed or intended method of getting from one set of circumstances to another. It is so simple. Do you want to get to another set of circumstances? If you are in a set of circumstances out of which you want to be extracted, you want to get to a better set of circumstances, do you not? Nobody wants to do worse.

Trust me, you are never going to do better without a plan. If you do not have a plan you are not going anywhere. That is what these lessons are designed to do, help us with our plan. You have to decide who you are going to ride with and who you are going to let ride with you. There are two folk you ought not let ride with you: the low rider and the dirty rider…Is it unchristian to want more? I want to be better. I want to do better. I want more in life. I want more than I have. If you do not want what you have, I want yours. That is the desired outcome.

Hip Hop Is Not Our Enemy

The last verse shows the result of Philip riding with the eunuch. **And when they were come up out of the water, the Spirit of the Lord caught away Philip.** That lets you know you do not have the same assignment for the rest of your life. Some of you are on an assignment that is past due. You are through with that assignment. God sent you for a season to ride with somebody. You rode with them, you helped them spiritually, and now you are all in their business. Get out of their Kool-Aid. Once you ride with somebody and help them do better in life they do not owe you an explanation. They do not have to call you and report to you. They do not need your permission [for anything]. Once you get them to the place God assigned you to get them, get off.

Some people are in your life only for a season. Some people you will never see again. That is why you have to do the best you can to help as many people as you can because some of them are only placed in your life for a short time. Young people in high school, I promise you 85% of the people you consider your best friends today you will not see anymore after you graduate from high school, if you graduate from high school. The one you are thinking about laying down and having sex with right now, the one you are all nervous, itchy, tingly, and twitchy about, you are not going to see them anymore. I know you do not want to believe it. Some people are only in your life for a season. There is nothing worse than somebody staying past their season. The reason you ride with people is so that both of you can be better at the end of the ride.

The Spirit of the Lord caught away Philip, that the eunuch saw him no more: and he went on his way rejoicing. The desired outcome of any relationship is that after we get through riding, for however long we ride, I am going to be rejoicing. Even in employment relationships where you do not like anybody and they do not like you, you do not have to like them during the ride as long as you are rejoicing at the end of the ride. When the eunuch told Philip to ride with him, they did not know each other. All Philip knew was here was a tall, effeminate-looking Black man that God told him to ride with. Some of you are turning folk off because of what you see on the outside. You better start listening to what God is telling you about the inside.

Some of my best friends were the kind of people that nobody wanted to do anything with in public, that people shunned, talked about, lied on, and laughed at. They were the people that poured into my life and gave me the benefit of their wisdom. Some of the people you would laugh at are the ones who opened up to me and allowed me to receive some of the wisdom that God had given them. There are people who have pure gold on the inside but do not look like anything on the outside. You better stop looking on the outside and start to see the heart. God is trying to show you some folk who can help you make it to your destiny. You have to listen to God and stop listening to man. Even if they hurt you and break your heart, it does not matter about the journey. It is what happens at the end of the trip. If I have to cry all the way, at least by the time we get to my stop I am going to be rejoicing.

God is showing you some things and letting you know it might be time to get off now. People you ride with who do not appreciate your joy might just be trying to steal it. The reason Philip stayed on the chariot with that effeminate man is because he knew there was something in the man that was not apparent from the outside. The reason he rode with him even though he knew people were going to talk about him is because he was obeying the [?] of the Holy Spirit. He knew that if he did what God said, God would reverse the situation, take what was down and bring it up. He would turn the situation inside out. God specializes in reversals.

The eunuch went on his way rejoicing, the one people were talking about, the lonely one. You might be lonely right now. You stay on the ride because at the end you are going to be rejoicing. This is where the

Pentecostal folk dropped the ball. They think that the end is praising. They think the end is shouting, speaking in tongues, and having a good time in church. That is not what "rejoice" means. "Rejoice" is from a Greek word pronounced *kairo*. It means to be exceedingly glad. When was the last time you were exceedingly glad? Do you want to be exceedingly glad? It is like being drunk on glad.

You know how you get a ticket for driving under the influence? When you have had too much to drink you are so under the influence of the substance that you no longer control your actions, the substance does. When you are drunk on alcohol it is not you that is carrying out the motions, it is the alcohol through you. When you are exceedingly glad it is your joy that controls your actions, not you. When you are exceedingly glad, you can be glad in the midst of situations that do not lend themselves to gladness. You can find a good thing in any negative situation. You do not let opposition to steal your joy. You can find gladness in the midst of your struggles.

When this ride was over the eunuch was exceedingly glad. Was he still a tall, effeminate Black man with a high voice? Yes. That lets me know that God will let you be who you are and still be exceedingly glad. Were folks still talking about him? I'm sure. It did not matter what folk said about him because on the inside he was exceedingly glad. Oh [I wish for the day] when I can have a church full of folk who can be exceedingly glad despite their circumstances, in spite of what their families do. It begins with you. I declare you to say, "I am going to be *exceedingly* glad. It might be today. It might be tomorrow. Whenever it is-ha! Ha! Ha!"

If you cannot say that and laugh it is because your butt has been whooped. You have been whooped in the spirit. You cannot even prophesy your own future, claim your own victory. If you cannot open your silly mouth and proclaim your own future then you do not

Dr. Kenneth T. Whalum, Jr.

have what it takes to be happy. I want some folk around me that can make something out of nothing. I want some folk around me that are determined to have joy and do not care what the circumstances say. I am determined to have some folk around me that can fight through the situations [?].

"Rejoice" also means to be well and to thrive. You all thought it just meant to clap your hands, stomp your feet, and shout for joy. It means more than that. It means to be well. In other words you are not going to be sick anymore. You are not going to suffer from the sickness of depression anymore. You are not going to be sick in your mind anymore. You are not going to be sick in your heart anymore. You are not going to be sick in your spirit anymore. You are not going to be sick in your soul anymore. Be well.

Not only does it mean to be well; it means to thrive. If there is one thing that the devil hates it is a blood-bought-born-again-Holy-Ghost-filled-fire-baptized child of God that not only is glad and well, but has money in his pocket, success on his job, success in his family, success in his future, success in everything they put their hands to do. That means to thrive. Jesus died, was buried, rose on the third day, went back to the Father, and sent the Holy Ghost for you just like He did for me. The same Holy Ghost that I have and has me is the same Holy Ghost you have and that has you.

Who are you riding with? It might be time to stop the car and put them out. It is all about being happy, being well, and thriving because you decided to let the Lord ride with you. The third group of folk you do not need to let ride with you is backseat drivers. It is in Job 42. Job's friends, Elephaz, Bildad, and Zopha, were backseat drivers. Folk are with you when everything is going all right, but as soon as you start going down through there is when you find out who your real friends are. Job started going down through there and he found that

Elephaz, Bildad, and Zopha were not really his friends. After the fact they became backseat drivers. Every last one of them went to telling Job how he must have done something wrong or God would not have been doing like He was doing. Have you ever known anyone who accused of being a liar when you say you trust and love God, you are trying to be holy, you are living celibate, and folk look at you, laugh in your face, and tell you that you are a liar? That is exactly what these three so-called friends did.

They started telling Job that he was lying on God, that God was not on his side, and not in his corner. They became backseat drivers after the fact, telling Job what he should do. Do you hate it when you let somebody ride with you and all of a sudden they tell you how you ought to go when you have been going the same way all your life? Do you get sick of folk riding with you telling you where the shortcuts are? They do not even have a car and do not know how to drive. Backseat drivers want to tell you how to live your life after they have messed theirs up. You better quit letting these backseat drivers get in the car with you. They will cause you to have an accident. Then there will be three folk's lives messed up: the backseat driver's, yours, and the one you ran into. You have to stop listening to these backseat drivers. God blessed Job's friends in spite of what they did because Job prayed for them. The Bible does not say anything about Job's friends coming to the house after he was restored. Once you get to a certain state in life you do not even have to invite them anymore.

Sometimes backseat drivers are not even in the backseat. Sometimes backseat drivers are sitting in the front with you. Sometimes the one you promised to love, cherish, protect, and cover will steadily run their mouths, telling you which way to go instead of being quiet and trying to support you in the things you want to do.

It is time for you to change riders now. It is time to put everyone out of your life that is not trying to help you in pursuit of your goals.

"We Ride" Series Installment #4

It is important who you ride with. It is important who you develop a rhythm with. Every now and then the rhythm gets thrown off…Yeah, you are going to be down, you are going to lose a job, you are going to experience direction, but when you are riding with the right folk going the right way you can miss a step every now and then, but you know somebody is going to pick you up and carry you until you can carry somebody else. When God heals you it is not because He wants you to be well. It is because He wants you to heal somebody else who is not well. Every time God blesses you with money it was so you could have money to give somebody else when they needed it. Every time God brought you out of the darkness was not just because He wanted you to be in the light. He brought you out of the darkness so you could hold a flashlight for somebody else who needs to come out of the darkness. Everything God has done for you was for somebody else.

The reason Philip was in place to get on that chariot with the Ethiopian eunuch is because he had almost lost his life doing what God wanted him to do. Philip was almost killed for trying to do right for God. Because he was faithful to God, God delivered him from death, put him on a whole other level, put him in a situation where he had folk around him to help him do what he needed to do. He was in place when the eunuch needed him. If you let God bless you right and let Him use you, He will have you in a place with somebody else where they need help.

Who are you riding with? How are you feeling right now? Are you feeling like you are riding by yourself? Are you feeling like you are on this thing by yourself and there is nobody to help you? If that is how you feel you need to put a whole lot of folk out of the car. You do not even have to stop. Put the car in neutral. Let it roll down the hill.

The reason the eunuch was in a position to help somebody is because he had been faithful to God. Though he was tall, skinny, had a high voice, and acted like a woman, he did not let that stop him from going to Jerusalem to do what he needed to do. You cannot let folk stop you from doing what you need to do. I do not care how they talk about you or laugh at you, do not let them stop you from going to Jerusalem to do what you have to do. When you get to Jerusalem, find an altar, fall on your face, and bless God.

The reason the eunuch was in place when God needed him was even though he did not have the whole truth he had the most important part of the truth. He did not know Jesus yet, but he knew how to worship God. I have some gang bangers, adulterers, fornicators, and shawties that strip for a living in my congregation who do not know Jesus yet but know how to worship God. As long as you know how to worship God, God will place somebody else in your life that will help you get where you need to go.

The whole premise is that you have to watch who you are riding with. You the part of the *We Ride* video where Mary J. is standing on a rock and she has changed outfits from her riding clothes? There was nothing wrong with her riding clothes, but every now and then you need to change outfits. Every now and then there are small nuances you need to change in order to get where God wants you to be. God really wants you to be standing on the rock.

It is all right to ride every now and then, but you were not meant to ride forever. Every now and then you are supposed to get somewhere. When you get where you are going it is time to get out of your ride, stand on the rock of God's salvation, and realize that He wanted you to be where you are right now and enjoy His best in your life. There comes a time when the struggle is over. Just because you make it through one struggle does not mean you are not going to have some more struggles.

I want you to remember that part where Mary J. got to the rock and she had a whole new outfit on. The Bible said that if any man be in Christ he is a new creature. Old things are passed away. Behold, all things are become new. You have to put on a new attitude and a new aptitude. In other words you have to stretch your thinking, capacity, limits, future, vision, destiny, expectations, experience, being, arms and legs. You have to stand taller than you did the day before. You have to stand up on top of your situation. You have to stretch and stretch and stretch.

Remember when Mary got up on top of the rock she was not up there by herself. Right behind her was an orchestra. When you go through what you have to go through and get to where God wants you to be, He will send folk that you do not even know to help you live out the meaning of your life. While you are into the dispensation of God's goodness on your life the winds and waves will be blowing, but they will not be able to reach you. In the video the waves were dashing up against the rock, but it did not bother Mary J. and it did not bother the conductor or the orchestra. You have to know that if the Holy Ghost is conducting your orchestra it does not matter what kind of wind blows in your life. It does not matter how the waves try to take you down, if the Holy Ghost is your conductor, He has a piece of wood in His hand. It is called the cross of Calvary. As long as the Holy Ghost is conducting by the cross of Calvary, your situation will be all right. The waves will not take you down. The wind will not overcome you. You will be standing.

It is important who you ride with and who you let ride with you. Do you not know there are some more folk on that road who wanted to ride

Hip Hop Is Not Our Enemy

with that eunuch? It was a time of worship. It was a time when people were going up and down the road coming to and fro, to Jerusalem to worship. There are a whole lot of folk on the road. You cannot let everybody ride with you that asks for a ride. You cannot let everybody ride. Just because somebody is always in your face does not mean you have to let them ride with you. Just because somebody is always in your business does not mean you have to let that person ride with you. You have to make good decisions about who is going to be your friend, who you are going to spend time with, talk to, and roll with. You have to make better decisions with your life. You have to stop wasting time with these folk who do not mean you any good.

The eunuch was not complaining about riding by himself. He had everything he needed. When you have what you need you do not have to beg anybody to ride with you. When you have what you need you do not have to beg for any company. Nobody needs company just for the sake of having company. Every time you go somewhere you have to pay for somebody's meal. You have to put gas in somebody's car. Nobody is trying to go out like that. If you have to ride by yourself, ride by yourself doggone it. Buy yourself some new riding clothes and shoes. You do not have to waste your time.

There were some more folk on the road, but it was not until Philip asked the eunuch if he understood what he was reading that the eunuch decided to ask Philip to ride with him. Here is how you can tell who you should let ride with you: people who indicate interest in your future. Philip asked the eunuch if he understood what he was reading. That said a lot of things about Philip. First of all he cared what he was reading. Stop wasting your time with folk who try to dictate your future instead of trying to listen and see where you are trying to go. The eunuch engaged him and asked how he would understand if he had no one to explain it to him.

The second thing you have to do is ask questions of the folk who are trying to ride with you. You have to try to have folk with you who can help you get better. You do not need to try to have anybody ride with you that will help you stay in the same place. Nobody has time to stop by the side of the road all day long trying to figure out if you are going to ride. Let me ask you a couple of questions: Are you concerned about my future, yes or no? Are you able to help get me to my destiny? Yes? Come on.

This is what you need to ask the next person who is trying to get with you. Ask the first question: Are you concerned about my future? Wait for the answer. Let that person know you have time. If the answer is yes, ask them another question because they might be concerned about your future for what you can do for them. Some of you have folk hanging on. They are not trying to help you, they are trying to get what you have. They are not even trying to work for anything. They are trying to get what you worked for.

If they answer yes to the first question ask them if they can do anything to help you achieve your destiny. In other words, can you pour anything into my life? I am sick and tired of pouring into folk that cannot pour back into me. I do not mind pouring into you if you are going to turn around and pour back into me, but I do not have time to pour into folk that are not going to do anything with what I pour out.

If they can answer the first two questions in the affirmative, stop wasting time and get together. I do not mean romantically. Stop thinking with your flesh so much. That is why you have sex with a different person every week. What you are looking for is somebody to make you feel good. We do not need anybody to make us feel good. You can drink some hot tea at night with some cream in it and that will make you feel good.

Hip Hop Is Not Our Enemy

If you have an active imagination you can do a whole lot of stuff to make yourself feel good and none of them involve another human being. Get your mind out of the gutter. It is not about feeling good. If somebody identifies himself/herself as somebody who is concerned about your future and can do something to pour into your life and help you reach your destiny, you go on and hook up with them. You do what you can to spend more time with them.

Even if you are riding with the wrong folk God will give you another chance. Even if you hooked up with the wrong crowd God will spare your life. He will keep you safe. He will keep you from being killed out here. God will ride with you even when you have the wrong folk. God will let you do a correction maneuver.

You know how when you are driving you can nod off? It does not even have to be late at night. It just depends on what you did last night. You nod off and wake up to realize you are going into another lane of oncoming traffic. Instinct causes you to do a correction maneuver. In other words you correct the steering wheel just enough to get in the right lane.

God will let you do a slight correction maneuver in the middle of the ride. Nobody else even knows you went to sleep, but God will guide and direct your life when other folk think you have it going on like a pot of smoking neck bones, God will wake you in your spirit and you will realize you have been asleep all this time. He will let you do a slight correction maneuver and before you know it you are back in the right lane.

It sure feels good to realize that you were asleep and going in the wrong direction, but now you are awake and going in the right direction. It feels good to know that I once was lost but now am found, was blind but now I see. It was nothing but the grace of God that kept me. The grace of God never left me. It shielded me, protected me, raised me, placed me.

You cannot let the low rider, dirty rider, or backseat driver ride. You also cannot let the drive-by shooter ride. **Ephesians 6:16 Above all, taking the shield of faith, wherewith ye shall be able to quench all the fiery darts of the wicked.** Check the conversation of the people you spend a lot of time with. Do you have a drive-by shooter in the car with you? Are they always shooting fiery darts at somebody else?

I want you to think about your friends, the ones you spend a lot of time talking to. Do they spend a whole lot of time shooting fiery darts at other people? If you ride with somebody like that, they are going to mess around and get you involved in a situation that you did not intend to get involved in. Let me tell you how slick folk are. They will be talking bad, shooting fiery darts at folk and then ask you for your opinion. You are not halfway paying attention to what they are saying. They will say something really low-down about someone and say, "Ain't that right, girl?" You will say, "Uh, huh. Yeah, that's right."

Before you know it they have spread to the person that they were talking about that you do not like them either. You have to stop letting these drive-by shooters ride with you. Let me tell you something. If you are in a car with somebody and they drive-by shoot on somebody else, you can expect somebody else to drive-by shoot on you. You will have yourself caught up in a situation that you were not even responsible for.

Stop riding with these drive-by shooters, these folk that never have a nice word to say about anybody. They are always talking old low-down, nasty, ugly words about folk, saying low-down folk in authority and people they do not even know. You do not know Michael Jackson. You do not know if he has a nose or not. You are just talking because you are talking. So what if Britney Spears looks a mess with her panties off. You do not have to say anything about her. You do not even know that girl. I bet if she offered you a thousand dollars you would say, "Yes, ma'am. I'll take a thousand." You watch folk who always have something nasty to say.

Trust me. God is going to quench all the fiery darts. If you are riding with somebody who is shooting fiery darts when God quenches them, He will quench you too. I do not even see how some of you can marry some of these low-down folk. You have hooked up with somebody who does not have a lick of compassion. I do not know why you think that because they talk nice to you and nasty about everybody else you think they are not going to be nasty to you one day. When somebody shows you who they are believe them. You do not need to ride with anybody who never has anything nice to say. Find somebody to ride with who knows how to speak words of encouragement in other people's lives, words of hope, happiness, and healing into somebody's life.

Do not let the sleeper ride with you. There is nothing worse than having a long drive with somebody in the front seat asleep. You need somebody to have conversation with to keep you alert. They get in the car with a knapsack, pillow, blanket, comforter, pajamas, ear muffs, putting cucumber on their eyes. They have on some house shoes and are getting in with some earphones on. You need to stay at home in the bed. You do not need to go with anybody like that. Why would I pick you up? I need to stop by your house and take a nap.

Who wants to ride with somebody who sleeps through all the danger. You need somebody who is going to see up ahead for you. You need somebody paying attention to the road. Quit letting these sleepers ride with you. They are good for nothing, slobbering out of the side of their mouth and looking all crazy. If you are going to ride with me, take a bath and a nap and be ready to ride with me because I am ready to drive. I am not ready to rest. I am ready to roll. It is not time to rest. It is time to roll. I am sick and tired of riding with these sleepers.

I Thessalonians 5:6-8 Therefore let us not sleep, as do others; but let us watch and be sober. 7For they that sleep sleep in the night; and they that be drunken are drunken in the night. 8But let us, who are of the day, be sober, putting on the breastplate of faith and love; and for an helmet, the hope of salvation. God will keep your mind in perfect peace whose mind is stayed on Him, but you have to put it on. Stop letting these sleepers ride with you. Try to hang out with folk who are paying attention to what is going on in the world.

You ought to have folk riding with you who can engage in conversation about current events. God is bringing reversal in the body of Christ so that a few of us, a remnant are going to be the ones on the cutting edge as was prophesied in my life by Bishop G.E. Patterson before he died. He said, "You are on the cutting edge. Stay out front. Keep doing what you're doing." God is bringing about a change. It is not coming to sleepers.

"We Ride" Series Installment #5

There are times in your life when you cannot help who you are riding with. Some of us are riding with some folk that if we had a choice we would have put them out of the car right after they got in. Be encouraged because even when you are not in control of your situation God will control the situation for you. He will keep you in the situation and let you get out on the other side without suffering too much harm.

God will let you be with some folk and situations that would have killed you at another time in your life. God will condition you. Ask the three Hebrews: Shadrach, Meschach, and Abednego. They did not volunteer to go into the fiery furnace, but they had to just because that is what the circumstances called for. Sometimes circumstances will require you to associate with some folk that ordinarily you would not have anything to do with. Just put your seatbelt on and trust God.

You are in some situations with some folk that you want to get away from, but you cannot leave right now. Trust me, God is fixing it so that when the time comes He will let you know and it is not going to take long. God is going to tell you to go on the spur of the moment. I do not know what it means-a marriage, job, or other situation-but God says if you stay awake He will show you when it is time to move. God says if you pay attention He will show you the signs that He is about to reverse the situation for you. If you ride with God do not worry about having to ride with some other folk. Stay as long as the Holy Ghost says you have to stay.

On the other hand, you are busy hating folk you have to deal with, but they are the very ones with your blessing in their hand. The word says that when they got to a certain point on the road, the eunuch commanded the chariot to stop. In other words the eunuch was not driving the chariot. The eunuch was a man of authority. He had plenty of money. He had a driver for the chariot. The driver could not help who he was riding with, but he had to obey the eunuch.

The driver could not decide when to stop. He had to wait for orders from the eunuch. When the eunuch said to stop the driver had to stop, but the result of it was that the driver was blessed. Sometimes God will bless you for being obedient when the blessing was not intended for you in the first place. That is why you have to pay attention and stay faithful to the Plan.

Recap: **Everybody wants to find somebody they can "ride" with in life, somebody they can share this planet with. This is not referring to romantic relationships. To ride with means to be**

Dr. Kenneth T. Whalum, Jr.

hooked up with people of like minds, and to accomplish positive things together. It's about establishing a "rhythm" in life.

Rhythm = (1) a regularly recurring pattern of activity, for example, the cycle of the seasons; (2) a pattern suggesting movement or pace. The Plan *is* a RHYTHM. A plan is a proposed or intended method of getting from one set of circumstances to another. We have to be careful who we let ride with us in life. The following are people you shouldn't allow to ride with you:

1. *The* LOW Rider (Proverbs 29:23).
2. *The* DIRTY Rider (Psalm 24:3-6). You should allow people with clean hands and pure hearts to ride with you, because DIRTY Riders shall not ASCEND into the hill of the LORD, and they shall not STAND in his holy place.
3. *The* Backseat Driver (Job 42)
4. *The* Drive-By Shooter (Ephesians 6:16)
5. *The* Sleeper (1 Thessalonians :6-8)

The next person you do not need to let ride with you is the Excessive Talker. Some folk just talk too much. They do not say bad stuff or gossip; they just talk too much. You want to pull your hair out because they will not shut up. Have you ever been trying to drive with somebody in the car with you and they will not shut up? You are trying to get somewhere you have never been and they yap, yap, yap, talking their head off, and you want them to tell them to shut up.

We get close to that with our children when they get to the age when they ask, "Why?" all the doggone time. You tell them why and then thirteen "Why?"s later they are still asking why. It takes the Holy

Ghost to keep you from strangling that baby girl. Some folk just talk too much. I would rather have somebody that says a few words, but the words they say have deep meaning, than to be around somebody that is talking a mile a minute and when they get through talking they have not said anything.

Look at Matthew 6:7 **Matthew 6:7 But when ye pray, use not vain repetitions, as the heathen do: for they think that they shall be heard for their much speaking.** You have to stay away from folk that talk just to hear themselves talking. You can usually tell when the person loves to hear themselves talking. You tune them out and go on about your business, but every now and then just look at their face and watch their expression. Their expression says, "I'm really impressed with me, I tell you. I'm so smart I just can't stand myself." They do not say that, but that is what their expression says. They think that God hears them and that everybody else hears them because they talk a lot. It is not the volume or number of words you speak that matters, it is the depth of the words you speak.

Proverbs 10:14 **Wise men lay up knowledge: but the mouth of the foolish is near destruction.** You do not need to spend a lot of time associating with people who when it is time to lay up wisdom, to work out some kind of plan (to take an extra job to make some extra money to put in the bank so you can have something in your future, to research on the internet for scholarships for your children, to find free scholarships to further your own education, to do some things to try to make a difference in your future). It is not time to talk. It is time to lay up wisdom. A foolish person talks a whole lot and lays up nothing for the future.

Even in church you need to check the people out that you spend a whole lot of time with. After three years of friendship do they have anything to show? Are they any better off today than when they became friends three years ago? Do they have any more today than they had then? Are they any closer to their degree than they were then? Do they look any better? Does their kitchen still need working? They talk all the time and they spend very little time laying up wisdom, planning for the future.

The mouth of the fool is near destruction. You can have folk in church who are not going anywhere. I want you to consider the people who you consider yourself friends with in the church. Do they show any signs of getting better? Are they growing at all? Are they always looking to you for direction and you have none yourself? Do they talk all the time and never lay up wisdom, lay up things for the future. Do not always gravitate to the folk who have a lot to say. It is not the number of words that matters it is the depth of the words that they speak. Do not let excessive talkers ride with you because they will make you have a wreck. As soon as you have a wreck in your life they will blame you. They are not going to help you when it is time to help. They are just going to talk.

One more person you cannot let ride with you is the hitchhiker. 1 Peter 5:8 **Be sober, be vigilant; because your adversary the devil, as a roaring lion, walketh about, seeking whom he may devour.** In other words the devil in the form of some of these folk you are dealing with is seeking whom he may devour. You have to stop picking up stray folk in your life. Stop letting other folk bring stray folk to you for you to straighten their life out. Please hear me. You have to stop letting other folk bring stray folk into your life and dropping them on you while they go about their business. The devil as a roaring lion walketh to and fro seeking whom he may devour.

The stray folk you are dealing with are trying to devour your life. You cannot send good money after bad money. You cannot cast your pearls before swine. You cannot allow people who are not pouring into your life to suck stuff out of your life. Do not let folk drain you of your life who cannot pour back into your life. Do not pick up folk who have no destination. Hitchhiking used to be very prevalent. You would ask them where they were going and they would ask you where you were going. Some folk just want to ride with you because they recognize you are going somewhere.

When you were struggling, did not have anything, were nappy-headed, did not have any money, could not afford lunch, and no one paid you any attention. Now all of a sudden you have some money, you can go get some weave put in every two weeks, and people are trying to spend time with you. Look at your present set of friends and see who has been there since then. Look at the folk you deal with and see who has been with you through the hard, rough times, when you went through hell and high water, the people who stuck with you when you did not have anything, who stood by you through thick and thin. Those are your real friends. Do not look at these Johnny-come-lately folk who did not come on until you got some money in your pocket. Those might be the hitchhikers that are trying to devour your life. Do not pick up hitchhikers.

If a person has been loving and serving God for any appreciable length of time God is going to bless them to have something in their lives. What are waiting on God for? He is not going to send you a check to the mailbox if you will not even go look for a job. Some of the hitchhikers you let ride with you have more than you have. They just do not want to spend their stuff on themselves. They want you to spend on them while they spend on what they want. You cannot let spiritual hitchhikers ride with you. You have to be sober and vigilant. You cannot get so desperate that you just get with anybody.

You have to stop watching the movies that are showing all the skin. You have to stop going to the places that remind you of what you cannot have. Quit dialing the 1-800 numbers and 1-900 numbers. Stay away from situations that remind you of your sin. Trust God to send you folk that you need to be with instead of folk that you want to be with. Do not let hitchhikers ride. As a matter of fact, pay attention to where you meet folk. If you meet them in church you have to watch them then. There are some shysters up in here now. There are some charlatans up in here now. I am talking about some fake-phony-baloney-pseudo-semi-slappy-head-saints.

You have to be careful who you associate with. Just because they speak in tongues does not mean that is the tongue of the Holy Ghost. On the other hand, if you are not even comfortable with your own relationship with God enough to receive His baptism to allow you to speak in his language, who are you to be suspicious of somebody else? God is not going to hurt you. Our congregation gave my wife Sheila and me a trip for our anniversary. The week before the trip my youngest son Kameron passed out from dehydration, fell and broke his jaw when his chin hit the floor. I was asking the LORD to let him be all right so we could go on our trip. And the LORD did what I asked Him to!

By the way, the doctors said that if Kameron's jaw had hit the floor one fraction of an inch to the left or right he may have suffered brain damage! I said the LORD did what I asked Him to! That trip was important to me, but it was more important to Sheila. I put a lot of stuff on the back burner to tend to my wife because she is no hitchhiker. She did not stop me to ride. I stopped her. When you know who you want to ride with you go out of your way to ride with them. I made her pay attention to me. She was not trying to catch my eye. I was trying to catch her eye when we met.

Our congregation prayed for my son and his condition improved so quickly that we were able to go on the trip as planned. That is the power of prayer. That is because we have folk riding with us who believe in the power of prayer. She did not pick up any hitchhiker. I did not pick up any hitchhiker. Our congregation did not pick up any hitchhikers. We are sharing a common destination. You have to be willing to let the Spirit of God work through situations. I never would have thought my son would have broken his jaw at this time in his life, the time when he got a scholarship solely based on his ability to play the horn. The devil tried to steal what God had placed in place.

Look at how God works. Because of the folk we are riding with and the prayers of intercession that went up before God like incense, the prayers accelerated the healing process. It is important to ride with folk who can get a prayer through. We are not here by mistake. This is not an accident. What God did for me He will do for you.

Watch the stories that people tell you. We were in Canada and a man came up to me while I was putting gas in our rental car. He told me a long story about his family, how his car was right down the street and he had until 11:00 to raise however much money he needed. He offered to show me his ID. Hitchhikers have their story straight. Folk that are not going anywhere will tell you a long story. I reached into my pocket, got some Canadian quarters, and gave them to him. He thanked me and told me he was going to take care of his business. I went into the store to use the bathroom. When I came out the man was asking another man for some money. By the time I left, the same man that swore that he needed money to get his car fixed was buying a bottle of beer in my presence.

That just goes to show you, you cannot trust what folk say. You cannot always believe the stories people tell you when they try to hook up with you in your life. Do not pick up spiritual hitchhikers unless God sends you to get somebody. Trust me, there is always somebody out here who needs some help doing something. You cannot meet everybody's needs. Some of you are red-eyed and sleepy because you stayed on the phone, trying to talk somebody out of suicide. That same person is right out in the street today, acting a damn fool. Next time they call you, tell them, "Tell you what, baby, try it. Go ahead on." They will sober up so fast. I am not making light of suicide. I am saying that you know who you are dealing with. You want to commit suicide because your mama told you to come in at eleven. No, you are just spoiled.

That concludes the list of people you should not let ride with you. You also have to watch who you ride with. There are going to be times in life when you are not the one picking somebody up. There are going to be times in life when you need a ride. There are going to be times in life when you need assistance. You are going to need to get from one point to another. There is no shame in needing help, but you have to watch who you hook up with even in those times when you need assistance.

Do not get in the car with the rubbernecker. Have you ever been trying to get to work, there was a wreck on the side of the road that you are not even on, and your side is more backed up than the side where the wreck was? Do you know why it is like that? Everybody driving past that spot was trying to see what was going on. A lot of folk offer you rides. My little girls, do not get in the car with any of these folk who pull over to the side of the road. If you are on your way to school and some grown man asks you if you want a ride, tell him no. Philippians 3:13-14 **Brethren, I count not myself to have apprehended: but this one thing I do, forgetting those things which are behind, and reaching forth unto those things which are before, I press toward the mark for the prize of the high calling of God in Christ Jesus.**

In other words I am not spending a lot of time rubbernecking. I am not trying to see what is behind me. I am trying to see what is ahead of me. Stop hanging with folk that are always reminding you of your past. The devil is always reminding you of the times when. You have to stop. You have to check him. You need to remind him of his future in the lake of fire. If your past is not a good thing then look toward your future. If your yesterday was bad your tomorrow is going to be good. If you yesterday was good, your tomorrow will be better. If your yesterday was better, your tomorrow will be your best. Your best days are yet to come, but you cannot hang out with folk who are always looking in the rearview mirror.

I press. I forget those things which are behind. I have a really short memory. I am not by myself. I have a really short memory when it comes to my mistakes. Others remember my mistakes I made yesterday; I do not. How are you going to make progress when you are always dwelling on what you did wrong in the past? You have to forget those things. You do not just forget. I am sick and tired of folk who forget and then repeat. What good does it do to forget if you are going to repeat? You have to press, stretch, and focus on the prize that God has for you in your life. You do not want to ride with folk who are rubberneckers.

Do not ride with the iPod listener. John 10:27 **My sheep hear my voice, and I know them, and they follow me.** People who drive cars with an ipod in their ear cannot even hear an ambulance as it comes up on them. They cannot hear you blow your horn if there is something about to hit them. They are focusing on what they are listening to and not on their surroundings.

You cannot spend a lot of time riding with folk who are listening to every voice but the voice of God. The thing about ipods is they are personal programs. You can design your own program and listen to only the music you like. You have to stop riding with folk who are only focused on their own plans, their own future, and their own good. You need to always ride with somebody who can pour into your life and benefit you through your association with them. A person listening to an ipod is not thinking about anything but what they are listening to.

Stop trying to ride with folk just because you think they have something. Try to identify with folk who hear the voice of God and recognize Him. How do you know when somebody hears the voice of God according to John 10? They follow God. I am trying to give you a simple measure of how you can assess your relationships with the people you are dealing with. Do you want to be with somebody who does not follow God or do you want to be with somebody who does follow God? It is just that simple. Do not ride with ipod listeners, that person who is dedicated to his own program and listens to something other than God.

Do not ride with the cell phone talker. Some of you cannot drive without talking on the cell phone. So you know you cannot drive while talking on the cell phone, dialing, texting, hitting the blinker, turning, and stopping. Titus 3:1-4, 9 **Put them in mind to be subject to principalities and powers, to obey magistrates, to be ready to every good work, To speak evil of no man, to be no brawlers, but gentle, shewing all meekness unto all men. For we ourselves also were sometimes foolish, disobedient, deceived, serving divers lusts and pleasures, living in malice and envy, hateful, and hating one another. But avoid foolish questions, and genealogies, and contentions, and strivings about the law; for they are unprofitable and vain.**

Folk talking on the cell phone and trying to drive are not focusing on what they ought to be focusing on. If you are driving you ought to be focusing on driving. If you are talking on a cell phone and driving you are just like these people who were given to divers lusts, endless questions, things that do not matter. I am saying, do not ride with somebody who is not focused on the important things in life. Think about the conversation of the people you trust in your life, the people you are trying to hang with. If they are not focused on positive things then they are just like the people in Titus 3 who are foolish, disobedient, and deceived. Do not ride with those folk.

Do not ride with the getaway driver Romans 1:28-32 **And even as they did not like to retain God in their knowledge, God gave them over to a reprobate mind, to do those things which are not convenient; Being filled with all unrighteousness, fornication, wickedness, covetousness, maliciousness; full of envy, murder, debate, deceit, malignity; whisperers, Backbiters, haters of God, despiteful, proud, boasters, inventors of evil things, disobedient to parents, Without understanding, covenantbreakers, without natural affection, implacable, unmerciful: Who knowing the judgment of God, that they which commit such things are worthy of death, not only do the same, but have pleasure in them that do them.**

In other words you are riding with folk you know are doing wrong, but you are helping them do wrong. You cover for them when they do wrong. You ride with folk who cover for other folk who do wrong. You do not want to be with folk who help you do wrong. You do not want to be with somebody who is not going to tell you when you need to be told you are wrong. You do not want to spend a lot of time with folk who will let you be halfway, a coward, a fornicator, an adulterer, or a liar without calling you into accountability. They are going to drive the getaway car to get away from God and into the devil's hands. Do not ride with the getaway driver.

God is trying to tell you that some of your associations need to come to an end. I know it is difficult to let some people go, but you need to trust God to make a way for you. The Bible says I can do all things through Christ which strengthens me. That includes *all* things. If you are in a situation in your life right now where the people around you are the ones who are preventing you from either letting go of what you need to let go of or from taking hold of the things you need to take hold of, it is time to separate yourself from those persons.

"We Ride" Series Installment Finale

There is a saying that you have to keep the main thing the main thing and not get distracted on side issues. What happened with the Ethiopian eunuch was he finally got to the main thing because he let the right one ride with him. A lot of us are spinning our wheels. We are not even dealing with the main issues because we are dealing with wrong riders. Sometimes it breaks your heart to have to separate from some folk, but God is letting you know that now you can deal with the main thing.

<u>Recap</u>: **Everybody wants to find somebody they can "ride" with in life, somebody they can share this planet with. This is not referring to romantic relationships. To ride with means to be hooked up with people of like minds, and to accomplish positive things together. It's about establishing a "rhythm" in life.**

Rhythm = (1) a regularly recurring pattern of activity, for example, the cycle of the seasons; (2) a pattern suggesting movement or pace. <u>The Plan</u> *is* **a RHYTHM. A plan is a proposed or intended method of getting from one set of circumstances to another. We have to be careful who we let ride with us in life. The following are people you shouldn't allow to ride with you:**

6. *The* **LOW Rider (Proverbs 29:23).**

7. *The* **DIRTY Rider (Psalm 24:3-6). You should allow people with clean hands and pure hearts to ride with you, because DIRTY Riders shall not ASCEND into the hill of the LORD, and they shall not STAND in his holy place.**

8. *The* **Backseat Driver (Job 42)**

9. *The* **Drive-By Shooter (Ephesians 6:16)**

10. *The* **Sleeper (1 Thessalonians :6-8)**

11. *The* **Excessive Talker (Matthew 6:7 and Proverbs 10:14)**

12. *The* **Hitchhiker (1 Peter 5:8)**

Do not get in the car with:

1. The Rubbernecker (Philippians 3:13-14)

2. The ipod Listener (John 10:27)

3. The Cell Phone Talker (Titus 3:1)

4. The Getaway Driver (Romans 1:28)

Rhythm is a regularly occurring pattern in life, for example, the cycle of the seasons. As long as God delays Jesus' return, the cycle of seasons is going to remain the same: summer, fall, winter, and spring. That is how life is. You are going to have up days and you are going to have down days. You are going to have days when you feel like everything is snapping for you and you are going to have days when you seem not to be able to get out of a deep depression. There are going to be days when you do not feel like you are at your best, but remember it is cyclical and everything that goes around comes around.

If you have the right riders with you, the right people associated with you, you will make it through the down days just like you make it through the up days. You will identify that when God has you in an up period in your life it is not just for you. It is so you can help somebody else who is going through a down period in their life. When you are going through a down period in your life always remember that there is somebody around you who can help you make it through the darkness of your life.

You do not have to ride with folk that the Holy Ghost did not hook you up with. If you are with somebody who is pulling you down it is time right now for you to separate from that person.

MARY J. BLIGE
"We Ride (I See The Future)"
From the day To the night We ride We ride We ride
I see The future baby You and I Better with time
And it is What it is And I Just can't help it
And I felt What I felt No I just can't help it
I see the future, baby Me and you That's how we do

Do you get a sense of well-being from the people that you are associated with on a regular basis? Do you get a sense of positive well-being from the relationships that you have a choice over? Do you get a sense that you are leading an orchestra in setting forth what God has done for you and allowing you to lift and help other people as a result of the relationships that you have a choice over? Do you feel beat down after dealing with the people that you deal with on a regular basis that you have a choice over? You cannot choose the people that you work with, who are in your classroom, your parents, but in the relationships that you choose, do you get the sense that everybody is supporting you in fulfilling your destiny? Do you get the sense when you are dealing with the people that you are in relationship with, that they are going the same direction you are going? Do you get the sense that all of this time you are spending with these people is going to result in a good thing in your life?

Philip ran thither to him, and heard him read the prophet Isaiah, and said, Do you understand what you're reading? You see, it does not matter what happens to you if you are reading the right thing. If you are trying to find the answers to the right questions, it does not matter what happens to you because you are going to find the answer in the word that you trying to understand, but if you are riding with a lot of folk whose priority is not the same as yours, if their values do not match your values, and what is important to you is not important to them, then they are not ever going to facilitate you getting the answers to the questions that you need. This eunuch was trying to find the answer and because he let the right person ride with him, God sent somebody that could help him get to the bottom of the matter.

I do not want to spend a lot of time with folk who are helping me ask questions. I need some folk in my life that will help me get the answer to the questions that I already have. I do not need to wonder who I am as a result of being with you. I need to feel more secure about who I am as a result of being with you. I do not need you to make you feel bad about who I am. I feel bad enough about who I am. I want to be what God wants me to be and I need you to help me become what God wants me to be. So Philip, out of obedience to God, joined himself to the Ethiopian eunuch and asked him if he understood what he was reading. Do *you* understand what you are reading?

And he said, How can I, except some man should guide me? And he desired Philip that he would come up and sit with him. Do not underestimate the power of relationship between Pastor and people. If there is a man that can help guide you through the things you have to go through right now thank God. Philip could not guide the eunuch if he did not ask him to do so. Some things you need to willingly suspend in order to allow your Pastor to be what God wants him to be to you. You have to suspend the notion that he is just a man. Yes, he is just a man, but right now he is the man you are riding with. It is his job to help you understand what you are reading. You have to want to understand. You have to invite him into your mind, spirit, thoughts, life, not take over or be in your business, but you have to be willing to trust him to guide you in the right direction.

This is the main thing. **The place of the scripture which he read was this, He was led as a sheep to the slaughter; and like a lamb dumb before his shearer, so opened he not his mouth: In his humiliation his judgment was taken away: and who shall declare his generation? for his life is taken from the earth. And the eunuch answered Philip, and said, I ask you, of whom speaks the prophet this? of himself, or of some other man? Then Philip opened his mouth, and began at the same scripture, and preached unto him Jesus.**

I have often wondered why the eunuch was reading this passage of scripture. Remember the eunuch was a man that had been frowned upon all his life. He was a eunuch. He had been castrated at an early age. It set him apart from other people. He had feminine characteristics. He was tall, had long legs, no hair on his skin, and had a high pitched voice. Folk had laughed at him and talked about him all of his life and yet he is reading about a sheep being led to the slaughter.

Isaiah 53:1- NIV Who has believed our message and to whom has the arm of the LORD been revealed? He grew up before him like a tender shoot, and like a root out of dry ground. He had no beauty or majesty to attract us to him, nothing in his appearance that we should desire him.

This may be one reason why the eunuch was reading this particular passage. This passage is talking about Jesus and it says that he grew up before him like a tender shoot, and like a root out of dry ground. It may be that the eunuch was identifying with whoever this scripture was talking about. Whenever you are in a situation where you are standing out from the crowd, you do not seem to fit in anywhere, and you start to feel like you are by yourself, begin to search the scripture for something where you can feel some hope even though you are different from everybody else.

This eunuch must have felt like a root out of dry ground. He must have felt like somebody that nobody understood, somebody who was by himself in this world? Have you ever felt by yourself even in a room full of folk, even in a house full of children, even in a job full of noise? Do you feel like you stand out in the crowd? That is what God is trying to get you to. It is not that He wants you to ride with me so you can blend in. He wants you to ride with me so you can feel like a sore thumb, why you feel like a fish out of water. There is a reason for your pain today. This is why.

All these pictures we see of Jesus as a beautiful man with smooth skin, long, flowing, brunette hair, perfect beard contradict this verse that says there was nothing in his appearance that we should desire him. If you are feeling put upon by people because of your weight, height, uneven length in your legs, pimples, the fact that you do not have the kind of hair that you want to have, a wide nose, the fact that you are so skinny, so light-skinned, so dark-skinned, the fact that you cannot speak right, whatever your shortcoming is, Jesus is letting you know that is Him. He and you are eye-to-eye. He is saying, "You are just like I am and I want you to understand why I let you be like you are.

There are some of us who do not consider ourselves physically unattractive, no matter what people think about us. There are some of us who have a healthy dose of self-esteem. We feel like we are doing pretty good. As a matter of fact if we did any better we could not stand ourselves. Notice that I am speaking in a personal pronoun kind of way. Even when you think you have achieved a certain standard, look what happened. **He was despised and rejected by men, a man of sorrows, and familiar with suffering. Like one from whom men hide their faces he was despised, and we esteemed him not.** I do not care how well you think you are doing there is always going to be somebody hating on you.

I am trying to tell you why the Ethiopian eunuch needed somebody to explain to him. He had all the money he needed but still did not fit in. It does not matter how much money you have if you do not understand why you are going through what you are going through. God has a plan for your life. The reason He let you go through all that mess you went through was so you could get to the point where you knew who you belonged to and that God was the only One who cared about you. If you had to lose everything you own, it was so God could show you that it was not you at all anyway. It was me with you all the time. God is trying to show you that He can make you something beautiful in spite of folk hating on you.

This is what the man was reading on the road. Thank God for His word. **Surely he took up our infirmities and carried our sorrows, yet we considered him stricken by God, smitten by him, and afflicted. But he was pierced for our transgressions, he was crushed for our iniquities; the punishment that brought us peace was upon him, and by his wounds we are healed.** If you trust Him He will give you your answers.

We all, like sheep, have gone astray, each of us has turned to his own way; and the LORD has laid on him the iniquity of us all. Have you ever turned to your own way and God let you go on out there by yourself, then He was there when you got where you were going? [Illustration: photo of sheep crossing a road] Those sheep know where they are going, but they are going anyway and they are going with such a single mind that they are stopping traffic. You have to be so determined that you are going to pursue God's goal for your life that you do not care who you have to stop trying to get where they are going.

You need to get where you are going. The sheep know where they are going. Jesus went all the way and did something to make it so that you do not have to go to the slaughter, but you have to go through something in order to get to the place where Jesus wants you to be. Every sheep in that crowd is a different sheep, but you do not see one sheep in there rebelling. Why is it so important to ride with the right people? Even if one of those sheep did decide that they were not going to go, there are too many sheep going that way for you to turn around. That is why you have to watch who you hang with.

Quit running with folk that let you give up so easily. Quit running with folk who will let you do wrong when you know you are doing wrong. You need to be with some folk that are going the right way, they are going to do what God says, and even when you get off track they will keep pushing you.

[Illustration: photo of sheep being separated] [These sheep have been separated,] but still none of them has turned around. I am not going to turn around and I am not going to let anybody else who is with me turn around. We have somewhere to go. You have to go through because you have to get to where this is.

He was oppressed and afflicted, yet he did not open his mouth; he was led like a lamb to the slaughter, and as a sheep before her shearers is silent, so he did not open his mouth. You need to shut up sometimes. You do not need to tell folk your business so you can get somebody to pray with you. Just be quiet and go through. Be quiet and realize that even though you are going through something others are too. Do not open your mouth and let your future be known to the devil. I am just going to be quiet, let God lead wherever He is going to lead me, and as long as I am on His path I am going to be all right.

In the process you are going to be oppressed. Somebody is going to lie on you, press you down, or get you off track, but be quiet and do what God wants you to do.

You are going to be oppressed and afflicted. Folk are going to go out of their way to mistreat you, to try to set you up, to try to make it look like you did something you did not do. If you stay on the right road, there is a promotion on the other side of your demotion. There is an increase on the other side of your decrease. There is a new job on the other side of you getting fired. There is a new situation on the other side of the hell you have to go through. Just be quiet and keep going through. Just keep moving.

By oppression and judgment he was taken away. And who can speak of his descendants? For he was cut off from the land of the living; for the transgression of my people he was stricken. He was assigned a grave with the wicked, and with the rich in his death, though he had done no violence, nor was any deceit in his mouth. Stop looking for reasons why you are catching hell. If you have not done anything to anybody and have been trying to do right, you can look to catch hell and suffer for it. Do not look for folk who do not understand where you are going to pat you on the back and build you up, but you ought to get encouragement from folk you go to church with every Sunday and Wednesday.

There ought not be anybody who has a mood and does not feel like speaking on any given day. That is not a sheep; that is a goat. I need somebody to smile at me and let me know that no matter what I am going through, they are with me, we are riding together, whatever I need, they have it, if I need some money, they have some money, if I need some conversation, they can talk, but most of all I need them to let me know they are with me. Do you feel like anybody in your church is with you, knows what you are going through, and cares what you are going through?

Even though Jesus did not open His mouth, He did not get off track, He did not complain, He did not rebel, turn around, go against the will of God, follow the devil, fornicate, commit adultery, or do any of those things that we would consider great sins, He did not lie, cheat, blaspheme, convert to another religion-any of those things, but look what happened to Him in verse ten. **By oppression and judgment he was taken away. And who can speak of his descendants? For he was cut off from the land of the living; for the transgression of my people he was stricken. He was assigned a grave with the wicked, and with the rich in his death, though he had done no violence, nor was any deceit in his mouth.** Sometimes when you do everything right and make every good decision, sometimes it is still the Lord's will to crush you.

Olives cannot make oil until they are crushed. You are kicking against it, but you cannot be a blessing to somebody else if God does not press some ministry out of you. If God waited on you to minister when you feel like it you will wait until you get your bills paid, until you get your hair done, until you do not have to worry about certain things, until you retire, but God wants to crush you now. The beauty of your ministry is that you are able to minister in spite of being crushed right now. What God is doing for you is blessing others through your pain. When you do things right and God crushes you anyway, you ought to throw your head back and thank God.

The eunuch was feeling crushed and then there came Philip, right when the eunuch had the most questions. God will bring you light at your darkest point. There are some things you can take today that you would not have been able to take five years ago. It would have driven you crazy five years ago, but you understand that God is blessing you to be a blessing to somebody else. You know He is not going to kill you because He already killed Jesus for me. You are going to live out every inch, every minute of your appointed time on earth.

The devil is not going to defeat you before the end of your journey. The devil is not going to kill you before you finish doing what God told you to do. You might not feel like you have the money to carry out the dream that God placed in your heart, but God told me to tell you that no matter what you say or are going through, you are going to make it all the way to the end of what God says. You are going all the way because you are on that road and are not going to turn around.

God crushed Jesus so you could get ministry. This is what Philip preached unto the eunuch. He preached unto him Jesus-period. Jesus went through all of these things so that the eunuch could benefit from rejoicing. When you ride with the right folk you can rejoice. Because Philip and the eunuch obeyed God, two men went away rejoicing. Two men obeyed and it led to three things. It is good when one obeys, but when you can get another person to obey with you (not in love relationships, but in the relationships with folk you go to church with) [that is a good thing].

<u>Here are the three things twofold obedience led to.</u>

1. When they came up out of the water the Spirit of the Lord led Philip away. Obedience leads to <u>a spiritual catching away</u>. Trust me, when it is time to get out of the situation you are in, if you have been obedient to God, the Spirit of God will catch you up out of that situation. He is not going to send an emissary, or an agent, He is going to send the Spirit of God Himself to snatch you up out of that situation. Sometimes when the Spirit of God catches you up, you might leave some stuff behind.

Sometimes when God catches you up, your wig might come off, you might have to leave your wallet behind, you might lose a shoe, but wherever He catches you up and takes you to, you are going to have tenfold more than you had to leave behind, but you have to obey God. The Holy Spirit will catch you up and catch you away.

Sometimes the Holy Spirit will catch you away in a situation that you did not have to leave physically. Sometimes God will fix it so that your mind will be so focused on Him that you do not even hear what folk are saying around you. God will catch you away to the point where you are on a whole other level. People are watching you, waiting for you to cuss somebody out, give up, fall down and fornicate, but the Spirit of God has caught you away to a new level in your mind. That is because you have been obedient.

When you obey God, there is nothing God will not do for you. He will make a way for you to do stuff you never even dreamed of. You can do more than you ever imagined. God will turn stuff over trying to find you. God will turn situations around trying to make a way for you. God will lift you up so that folk will keep you up while you are trying to go down. God will fix it so that people will not let you fail because you have been obedient. Do not worry about what you are going through. God has you.

Sometimes you have to leave them for good. Sometimes you have to let them leave you for good. It does not mean that anybody has hard feelings, but it is just that some relationships are supposed to be over now. Folk are tripping about going to high school reunions. I am not going. The reason I made it now is because I quit having to deal with some of the folk I was having to deal with. Obey God. Let Him bring about some permanent separation. Some folk I am so glad I am never going to see anymore I could just shout every time I think about it.

Some folk I am glad not to be around anymore. You ought to be glad about that.

If God took somebody out of your life it was because you were ready for them to go. (Preach, pastor!!! ☺**)** If God let some folk go it means He was trying to prepare you to be moved up a level. There are some folk you are getting ready to meet that you could not have even dealt with before. There are some folk you are getting ready to meet who will facilitate your destiny because you are permanently separated from your negative past.

2. The eunuch saw him no more. That was <u>a permanent separation</u>. Some of you cannot really get where God wants you to be because you keep going back. You keep taking folk back in, giving them another chance. You want to be with somebody so bad you will accept anything. God is saying that some people are only in your life for a season. When He separates you, you have to let it be a permanent separation.

There are some family members who the last time you saw them is the last time you ought to see them. Some of the folk in our family are worse for us than demons themselves. God wants to cause a permanent separation. There is no need in you closing your eyes and looking back on the good old days. They were the good *old* days. God has some good new days waiting on you, but He cannot get you to your good new days until you let go of your good old days.

God is trying to catch some of you away right now. It feels so good to get caught away. I had to go to Texas to get caught away. When I got it I brought it back to Memphis with me. Because the Spirit caught me away he caught a lot of my congregation away.

3. <u>You get a "his way" rejoicing.</u> He went on his way rejoicing. Who went on his way rejoicing? It depends on how you read it. It is either the eunuch, Philip, or both of them. God can fix it so you can have an either/and/or life. God will fix it so you do not have to choose one good

thing over another good thing. God will fix it so you can have two or three good things and three or four good things waiting for you to get finished with those. God does not want to withhold any good thing from you. He will let you rejoice your way.

You do not have to rejoice my way. You might like buttered toast, shredded in a bowl with milk on it. That might not turn you on, but God will let you rejoice your way. Burger King had it right. You can have it your way. You can achieve what you want to achieve. God has a designer destiny for you if you obey Him.

Rejoice! That means to be exceedingly glad. Are you exceedingly glad? You can have your own personal way of rejoicing if you will just move into it. Frank Sinatra, Sammy Davis, Jr., and Tony Bennett did it their own way. Why can I not do it my way? I can be exceedingly glad if I obey God. Practice it right now. Just be glad. Be exceedingly glad your way. Do not worry about tomorrow. The trouble of tomorrow is going to take care of itself. Your gladness chases away your sadness. It chases away disease that tries to take up residence in your spirit. Because of your obedience [in being exceedingly glad], you will run away a lowdown thought that you were going to think about somebody. You will move into an area where you and Jesus are on the same level.

Rejoice also means to be well and to thrive. In other words when you get sick you are going to get well. If you are not sick you are not going to get sick. You are going to be well and thrive. If you expect to thrive, to not have to worry about money anymore, say so. Say, "I am going to be well, thrive, have more than enough, and be saved, sanctified, and filled with the Holy Ghost."

Why is that possible? It is because of what Jesus did that the eunuch was reading. He went and paid the price for all of us. Philip came and [explained who Jesus was, that He went through the crucifixion like a lamb to the slaughter, that He paid the price for his sin, and that all he had to do was except and receive what Jesus did for him and be baptized. Just at that moment when Philip was preaching Jesus they passed by a body of water on the side of the highway. Here is what the eunuch did not understand. You do not have to jump through hoops. You do not have to do anything extra special. You do not even have to speak in tongues to be baptized. All you have to do is find some water to be baptized.

If you have been baptized you have everything you need to be what God wants you to be. You do not have to read another book, go to another conference, watch another DVD, or get hands laid on by another preacher. If you have been baptized in the name of the Father, the Son, and the Holy Ghost, when you came up out of the water you came up with everything you need to be able to rejoice. Jesus went all the way for you so that you would not have to go there anymore.

Once the eunuch got the news he went away rejoicing. Philip also went away rejoicing because he was stupid enough and silly enough to do what God said to do. He was silly enough to be seen riding with a 'homosexual'. He was riding with an effeminate man. He was riding with somebody that nobody wanted to have anything to do with, but he did not care what people said. He was only trying to do what God wanted him to do. God is saying to you today that there is somebody who can be saved because of you. I want you to ride with them now.

LaVergne, TN USA
09 March 2010
175320LV00002B/46/P